BECOMING A
STEWARD
LEADER

BECOMING A STEWARD LEADER

FUNDAMENTALLY CHANGE THE WAY YOU THINK, LEAD, AND LIVE

CHRISTIAN LEADERSHIP ALLIANCE

EDITORS • MARK L. VINCENT • JOSEPH KRIVICKAS

CHRISTIAN LEADERSHIP
ALLIANCE

Becoming a Steward Leader: Essential Insights from Stewardship Thought Leaders and Practitioners.

Executive Editor of the *Nonprofit Leadership in a For-Profit World* series: Joe Krivickas, CEO SmartBear Software, Chairman and Founder of the Gordon College Center for Nonprofit Studies and Philanthropy.

Becoming a Steward Leader Editor: Mark L. Vincent, Ph.D., CCNL, CEO/Senior Design Partner, Design Group International.

Foreword by Dan Busby, CEO Evangelical Council for Financial Accountability.

Afterword by David Lose, Assistant Professor of Homiletics, Luther Seminary.

ISBN 13: 978-1-4141-2258-8
ISBN 10: 1-4141-2258-6
Library of Congress Catalog Card Number: 2011961728

DEDICATION

This volume is dedicated to the hard-working and faith-filled people who delayed building their homes until their churches were built; who established, prayed for, and supported ministries that offered the gospel for soul and body; who built schools to train young men and women to be Christian leaders in their chosen vocations; and who bequeathed their estates so that even more might be done for those who came after them. May the Spirit that rested on them fall on us seven-fold.

CONTENTS

INTRODUCTION TO THE *NONPROFIT LEADERSHIP IN A FOR-PROFIT WORLD* SERIES.

The *Nonprofit Leadership in a For-Profit World* series is released in association with the Christian Leadership Alliance and Azusa Pacific University and covers the main themes of equipping Christian leaders as they work on the front lines, serving those in need.

Top priority has been given to contemporary issues, some of which may not be dealt with elsewhere from a biblical point of view. The series aims to bring the best practices of organizational excellence reworked through a Christ-centered worldview. It is intended to be of value to Christian leaders at all levels, whether serving in a parachurch, a church, or in secular organizations. It should appeal to those who are educated lay-people or biblically trained.

The topics covered in the series are not exhaustive but have been chosen in response to modern-day thinking. In offering the series, the authors and the publisher hope that it will bring honor to Christ by being a tool that His servants can use as they serve within His kingdom.

—**Joseph K. Krivickas**
Series Editor

FOREWORD

By Dan Busby

Horace Bushnell is credited with saying, "One more revival, only one more is needed; the revival of Christian stewardship; the consecration of the money power of the Church unto God; and when that revival comes, the Kingdom of God will come in a day. You can no more prevent it than you can hold back the tides of the ocean."

While the theology and practice of stewardship are essential components of the Christian faith and Scripture is clear that Christians are called to be stewards of the gospel of Jesus Christ to complete the Great Commission and practice the Great Commandment[1], it seems that few Christian ministries today are comfortable with the biblical topic of stewardship. As a result, many of the resource-raising efforts of Christian organizations today look very much like the secular ones.

As Philip Yancey notes in his book *Finding God in Unexpected Places,* after reviewing the sixty-two fundraising appeals he received in a month's time, he concluded that appeals from Christian organizations

---

[1] For more on this subject, see the chapter from Mark L. Vincent.

used the same transactional techniques (underlining, use of post scripts, and focus on urgency) as everyone else and that not a single appeal from a Christian organization focused on Yancey's need as a Christian to honor and obey God through his giving.[2]

Similarly, Denver Seminary Distinguished Professor of New Testament Craig Blomberg, in the book *Revolution in Generosity*, raises the core issue: why is it that "Christian ministries that are raising money do not stress the central Biblical truths that giving is a part of whole-life transformation, that stewardship and sanctification go together as signs of Christian obedience and maturity, and that God will call us to account for what we do with 100 percent of the possessions He has loaned us."[3]

Both Yancey and Blomberg are correct—that most Christian ministries have adopted the "whatever works" approach of the transactional concept of most fundraising programs. However, generosity is not happening when the general population is giving barely 1 percent per capita and the most generous group—evangelicals—are barely giving 4 percent per capita. In general, Christians want to avoid the topic of faith and finances. Most seminaries are not teaching on the topic, and pastors are avoiding it like the plague. As a result, fundraisers from Christian organizations have joined the path of our culture in raising resources.

So a crisis exists. There is a lack of generosity due to denying that wise stewardship and generous giving are the natural outcome of a life devoted to God and Christ. It is through God's transforming a person's heart to reflect the image of Christ that he or she becomes generous as Christ is generous.

Becoming a Steward Leader: Essential Insights from Stewardship Thought Leaders and Practitioners addresses these concerns for the lack of generosity and the lack of spiritual focus discussed by Philip Yancey and Craig Blomberg by providing a primer on stewardship that will assist organizations to shift their focus from solely asking for support to helping Christians be rich toward God by honoring God with their possessions.

From its formative years, the Evangelical Council for Financial Accountability's (ECFA's) standards have been based on a biblical

---

[2] See Rebekah Basinger's chapter.
[3] See Wes Willmer's chapter.

worldview that relies on the truth of God's Word as the authority. The basis for this position is found in 2 Corinthians 8:12: "For we are taking pains to do what is right, not only in the eyes of the Lord but also in the eyes of man."

As you look at the ECFA standards, there are three basic areas that constitute the concerns of accountability: governance, finances, and fundraising/stewardship. *Becoming a Steward Leader* concerns itself with this third area and is addressed, in particular, to those in ministry who desire to raise resources from a biblical worldview. ECFA believes that as organizations adhere to standards of accountability, this results in organizational credibility that fuels generosity from the constituents, which in turn funds Great Commission efforts.

Becoming a Steward Leader builds on many previous steps ECFA and Christian Leadership Alliance have taken to provide resources in this area of stewardship. In 2003, ECFA joined in an effort to look at a biblical worldview for raising resources. A taskforce of twenty-three individuals (including three seminary presidents) were assembled under the leadership of Wesley K. Willmer (then a vice president at Biola University). This group developed the Biblical Principles of Stewardship and Fundraising document. ECFA published these principles, which were among the early documents advancing a biblically-based movement that emphasizes the primary purpose of fundraising as raising people to be rich toward God.

As a further development of these principles, biblical stewardship is based on these three assumptions:

1. Giving generously is not predicated solely on the work of an individual or an organization's efforts but rather on God's work in people. First Corinthians 3:6–9 reminds us that though we sow and cultivate in people's lives and may have the privilege of reaping, God is the One who makes things grow.[4]

2. It is a transformed heart that is generous as a person conforms to the image of Christ, who is generous. Scripture shows us the stark contrast between the true generosity of Barnabas (Acts 4:32–37) and the imitation generosity of Ananias and Sapphira (Acts 5:1–11).

---

[4] See Gary Hoag's chapter.

3. Resource-raising from a Christian perspective is not solely about securing transactions or gifts; rather, it is about encouraging spiritual transformation—helping people become givers, rich toward God. In Philippians 4:17, the apostle Paul said, "Not that I am looking for a gift, but I am looking for what may be credited to your account." Paul cared about what was happening in the hearts and lives of the Christians in Philippi, regardless of whether or not they gave.[5]

In *Becoming a Steward Leader*, the authors were asked to condense a significant aspect of their work to a single chapter, answering the question of what they would say about the subject to which they dedicated their lives if there were but one remaining opportunity and mere moments to do so. In short, if there were just one book to read on the subject, this primer on stewardship would be it.

It is my earnest prayer that God will use this book in a significant way to raise, from a biblical worldview, the necessary resources to fund ministries and fulfill the Great Commission.

Dan Busby
President, ECFA

Dan Busby is president of ECFA (Evangelical Council for Financial Accountability), the leading accrediting organization for churches and other religious organizations. He is also a noted author and speaker.

---

[5] See the chapter written by Natalie and Leslie Francisco.

INTRODUCTION TO *BECOMING A STEWARD LEADER: ESSENTIAL INSIGHTS FROM STEWARDSHIP THOUGHT LEADERS AND PRACTITIONERS*

onsumerism is winning. People do not want to contribute to government by the people, but they want the benefits of the government being for the people to continue to flow. People do not think first of what they will leave to their children but rather about the inheritance they will receive when their parents are deceased. People look at a congregation as a place that will serve them rather than the centerpiece of their service. People want the cheapest prices for the goods they buy without consideration of the social, environmental, or human costs paid behind the scenes.

Teaching people generosity flies in the face of teaching them to be consumers. Generosity is what saves the lives of widows and orphans, brings recovery of sight to the blind, frees people from the prisons of body and mind, gives homes to the homeless, and provides hope for those once hopeless. The urgency of recovering the intentional teaching and expectation of generosity is before us and makes the publication of this book most timely.

While there are many credible and significant voices in biblical stewardship, this particular assembly of people is at the top of the list. This is not just because of what they have written or where they have led, but because one or more of the following are present in their bodies of work:

- What they write and teach influences a developing body of literature that is being taught in congregations *and* institutions of higher education.
- What they practice personally and as organizational leaders keeps resulting in new and sustainable ministries with a global impact.
- They are at the forefront of instructing others in both biblical stewardship and how it is applied in inviting support for ministry.
- They have been particularly concerned with growing the heart of the giver over the funding of institutions.
- They understand the local church as the molecule that constitutes the body of Christ and are deeply concerned with developing generosity as a key practice of disciples of Jesus Christ.
- They keep advancing the idea of the life of the steward as a motif for how a leader leads an organization.
- They are recognized as thought leaders, examples of stewardship practice, or both.

In this book, we ask seven such people to distill their work into a single chapter. We asked them this question: *if you had just one opportunity to convey what you are learning about stewardship in a single chapter, what would you say?* Each author found this a challenging exercise, but they also reported how it helped them advance their thinking. That means that while some readers will find this book to be a good collection of material not previously gathered in one place, others will find it to be a wake-up call to think about their lives as steward leaders. All who read this book will find new and challenging insights for them personally and as leaders of organizations.

We opted to let each person speak with his or her own voice rather than trying to lay down editorial barriers that forced all of the material into a common sieve. This means there are different chapter lengths and different ways in which material is presented. You will find some differences in terminology. You may notice these authors might disagree about how much one gives away and what one does with his or her estate while he or she is alive. Even so, each one is well into the journey of baptizing his or her wallet and agrees that this is an arena where one is never done learning and growing, inviting you to come along on the journey.

This book provides a specific and intentional progression of ideas for steward leaders. *This progression shows us where we are in relationship to where we want to be, reminds us where we want to be, and then helps Christian nonprofit leaders begin to go there.*

Chapter One: Wes Willmer, long known for advancing biblical stewardship, provides an overview of changes in stewardship understanding and practice in American history, ending with how matters stand today and what we might do next.

Chapter Two: Developed from a long-time practice in helping congregations and ministry organizations get their minds right around money and faith, I bring together the basic biblical description of the life of a steward, the god-like power of money that the steward leader must wrestle to the ground, and how these understandings can be passed along.

Chapter Three: Bishop Leslie and Natalie Francisco, pastors who have planted churches on several continents, describe the essence of their teaching about giving as an essential discipline of Christian living that funds the local church and ministries beyond. The Franciscos teach tithing principles globally and without the apology so many other clergy feel must be given.

Chapter Four: Scott Rodin distills his increasingly recognized work on the process of how the life of the steward translates to becoming a steward leader. This is not just theology because he has applied it in many organizational situations as President, CEO, and consultant.

Chapter Five: Gary Hoag draws from his experience as a development professional and a New Testament scholar to apply the function of a steward leader to the vocation of inviting support for ministry.

Chapter Six: Rebekah Basinger, whose research with Thomas Jeavons influenced many to begin thinking about fundraising as ministry, describes how the steward leader grows the heart of the giver.

Chapter Seven: Gary Moore, a financial and investment counselor for many people and organizations, provokes us to think about how the steward leader participates in the economy at large.

This book, like the other volumes in the series, are designed for individual reading and growth, but they perform even better when used as part of a conversation with other leaders who are reading them at the same time. Perhaps you are in a networking group, a management team, or board that would benefit from group discussion across several meetings. Working through this material also provides good content for a leadership retreat. Each chapter invites you to ask and answer the following questions:

- Is this what I believe? If not, what is it I do believe?
- Is this my practice? If not, what is my practice?
- Does my organization operate with these understandings? If not, by what understandings do we operate?
- Are we improving the overall understandings and practices of the life of the steward, or are we just taking the results of other people's work?

May God speak to you as you read and reflect on what is provided in these pages. And may you find your heart for generosity grows even as you invite this growth in others in the face of rampant consumerism.

—Mark L. Vincent
Kohler, Wisconsin
New Year's Eve, 2011

1

THE SHIFTING MOTIVATIONS FOR GIVING AND ASKING: WHERE HAVE WE COME FROM, AND WHERE ARE WE GOING?[6]

BY WESLEY K. WILLMER, PH.D., CCNL

We like to think of America as a generous nation and its people as generous. The publicity of multimillion-dollar gifts and news that giving exceeds $300 billion gives the impression of generosity. The giving in the US is more than any nation, and we are moving into a time when the largest transfer of wealth in the history of the US may take place.

Sociologist Arthur C. Brooks called America a "nation of givers," and compared to the rest of the world, America stands out in giving, but how did we become this way? Research shows that fervency of faith is what drives generosity in America. The more active people are in church activities, the more generous they are in volunteering time and money. While the general population gives on average 1 percent per capita of its income, as a whole, Roman Catholics give 1.5 percent, mainline Protestants give 2.8 percent on average, and Evangelical's donate almost 4 percent of their income. Does that sound generous?

---

[6] This chapter is adapted from *God and Your Stuff*, chapter 6, by Wesley Willmer with Martyn Smith, copyright 2002. Used by permission of NavPress, all rights reserved. www.navpress.com.

While the largest recipient of giving is religion, "The Charitable Behavior of Americans" study indicated that 73 percent of all contributions given to charities other than religion come from the same group that supports religion and claims religious membership and involvement. The study further notes that the local church congregation bears the brunt of responsibility for transmitting the spiritual and moral underpinnings that motivate individuals to give.[7] And yet, as Christians in the United States (about 86 percent of the population) have made more money, their giving has steadily declined in real terms.[8] If we look at the big picture of cultural change and motivations for giving, it appears that the patterns of the past are quickly moving away, and the motivations for giving are quickly changing. Is it possible that giving as we know it is a thing of the past?

As you know, we live in an age of incredible change! With or without our realization, these changes are significantly influenced by the forces of the culture around us. Never in our lifetimes have the fundamental institutions that govern and shape our society been held in such disrepute. The traditional family, government, education, and virtually every other social institution, including the church, and the values of these institutions are quickly eroding. As Randy Alcorn states, "In the Christian community today, there is more blindness, rationalization, and unclear thinking about money than anything else."[9]

These cultural changes have also radically influenced how we give and ask for money. The purpose of this chapter is to examine some of the cultural shifts of the last 270 years in terms of our motivations for giving and how we ask for gifts. As George Santayana said, "Those who cannot remember the past are condemned to repeat it."

Just as today's culture became more materialistic and redefined itself without God, culture also redefined our use of possessions without God. Much of the Christian church has failed to follow God's blueprint when it comes to our possessions. As a result of this condition, God's Word is diminished, our souls are not growing as they should, and the church's ability to witness to the world is weakened.

---

[7] See the chapter from Bishop Leslie and Natalie Francisco.

[8] John and Sylvia Ronsvalle, *The State of Church Giving Through 2005*, empty tomb. orghttp://www.emptytomb.org/table1_05.html.

[9] Randy Alcorn, *Money Possessions and Eternity* (Wheaton, IL: Tyndale House, 1989), 21–22.

Evidence of this decline is that: (1) Christians are failing to reverse the culture.[10] (2) Christians have become theologically thin.[11] (3) Giving to denominations is declining.[12] (4) Church-attendee giving per capita is declining.[13] (5) Poor use of possessions is having a negative effect on all giving,[14] growing compartmentalization between faith and finances[15] and a growing concern for a decline in all of giving.[16]

In addition, materialism is increasing; churches, seminaries, and colleges seldom address the biblical stewardship issues of faith and finances; and debt is at an all-time high. Issues of greed are at the core of the financial recession and tie in with the concern of the occupy Wall Street demonstrations. Furthermore, eight out of ten Christians do not give at the 10 percent level, do not believe they could give at that level, and do not have the practical knowledge needed to give at that level.[17]

How did we get so far off the path? How did we get derailed and blinded on this subject so vital to God? This cloud of confusion has come upon us with a slow trajectory—journeying down a seemingly similar path that continues to diverge, until we—too late—discover we are irretrievably lost. I have found in my life that once I understood the cultural forces that put us on the wrong trail, I was able to start to alter my course. Unfortunately, little has been written about the long-term influence of a changing culture on our motives for use of possessions. To gain this perspective, it is helpful to see how attitudes have changed over time.

---

[10] Nathan Hatch, "Can Evangelicalism Survive Its Success?" *Christianity Today* (October 5, 1992, 36) and Mark Noll, *A History of Christianity in the United States and Canada* (Grand Rapids, MI: Eerdmans, 1993).

[11] David Wells, "Lengthening Shadows and Peril Over Evangelicalism" at the annual convention of the National Association of Evangelicals, 1992.

[12] John and Sylvia Ronsvalle, *Behind the Stained Glass Windows* (Grand Rapids, MI: Baker Books, 1996).

[13] John and Sylvia Ronsvalle, *The State of Church Giving through 1998* (Champaign, IL: Empty Tomb, Inc., 2000).

[14] Robert Payton, "God and Money," In D. F. Burlingame, ed., *The Responsibilities of Wealth* (Bloomington, IN: Indiana University Press, 1992).

[15] Robert Wuthnow, "Pious Materialism: How Americans View Faith and Money," *The Christian Century* (March 3, 1993).

[16] Robert Wuthnow, Virginia A. Hodgkinson, and Associates, *Faith and Philanthropy in America* (San Francisco: Jossey-Bass Inc., 1990).

[17] George Barna, *The Mind of the Donor* (Glendale CA: Barna Research Group, 1994).

We did not simply wake up one day to find that the economic values of our culture had changed. The values we live with now come from a long period of cultural shifts. A good place to start is to understand this slide from the perspective of American history. Peter Dobkin Hall's book *Inventing the Nonprofit Sector*, as outlined by David McKenna,[18] traces the turning points over the past 270 years and shows us how we arrived where we are today: that our charity—or what we do with our stuff—is inseparable from our culture, our character, and our souls.[19]

Two basic questions help direct us through the journey of understanding the influence of cultural change upon our use of possessions: "why?" and "how?" A fundamental starting point is that there are three primary motivations for giving: 1) benefit to us personally; 2) help for others; and 3) stewardship to God. While all of these motives may entwine in our giving, it is assumed that one of the three will be the driving force behind our gifts and answer the question, "Why do we give?"

Over the past 270 years, our giving philosophies toward possessions kept shifting. These shifts reflect the changing answer that our culture gives for the question, "Why do we give?" There are four main eras that we consider in this chapter:[20] 1) Stewardship, 1740–1840; 2) Philanthropy, 1850–1950; 3) Development/Self-centered, 1950 to the present; and 4) Big Government—current. While recognizing that these ways of giving entwine and overlap in our history, one of these three answers dominates within each period, and one of them may well reflect your attitude today.

THE STEWARDSHIP ERA, 1740–1840

While it is debatable to call the United States a "Christian nation" (even though 87 percent list themselves as Christians), the fundamental fact is that the US has deep Christian roots. Such phrases as "endowed by our Creator with certain inalienable rights" and "In God We Trust" are not idle words. Personal and corporate faith in God permeated the lives of US founders with the attitude and motive of biblical

---

[18] David McKenna, "Giving is Not Guaranteed." Keynote speech to Christian Stewardship Association, September 20, 1992, Indianapolis, IN.

[19] Peter Dobkin Hall, *Inventing the Nonprofit Sector* (Baltimore, MD: Johns Hopkins University Press, 1992).

[20] These eras cross over each other at points, and vestiges of certain periods show up in others, but the trend lines are accurate.

stewardship. They believed that: (1) God provides all resources; (2) God trusts humans with the responsibility to manage these resources; and (3) God holds each one accountable for the way in which he or she uses these resources. To our Puritan ancestors, in particular, money was significant among the resources to which they applied the stewardship test. This attitude became so pervasively engrained in early American culture that the Stewardship period continued from the founding of our nation into the 1850s; and traces of it are still visible today, such as the attitudes expressed by E. W. Matthews when he wrote:

> The Christian life does not consist in going to Church and keeping the commandments, and so getting to heaven because of faithfulness to certain forms; it means that "life is a trust, a stewardship." That was our Lord's idea of being faithful, an idea we have pitifully narrowed. He did not talk of being faithful to creed or commandment, but of being faithful to what has been committed to us. Life is not a probation that ends in reward or punishment in another world; it is a power and a possession which we are to use. God has made us working partners in his plan for the world. The New Testament word is "Stewardship." The modern word would be "partnership" or "trusteeship." Stewardship has many sides. There is the stewardship of time, which demands that one's time be so used that it shall count most for God's great end. The stewardship of business requires justice and love for men in the shop and on the street; it asks how we are making our money. The stewardship of money also concerns the spending of money. In the Christian use of money, the fundamental fact is not tithing but stewardship.[21, 22]

This Stewardship period was built on three intertwining roots: (1) the ideological root of biblical stewardship; (2) the democratic ideal of the common good; and (3) the Puritan ethic of responsible piety.

The ideological root of biblical stewardship was brought by our founding forefathers and mothers, who had a biblical vision for the moral community, which made personal redemption and social responsibility inseparable. Just before the Pilgrims disembarked from the Mayflower to establish the Plymouth Colony, they heard this biblical

---

[21] E. W. Matthews in "Woman's Home Missions of the Methodist Episcopal Church," Volumes 37–38, February, 1920, p. 49.
[22] See Mark L. Vincent's chapter for a more detailed discussion on the tools of stewardship.

vision enunciated in a sermon by their governor, John Winthrop. He preached:

> We must delight in each other, make others' condition our condition, rejoice together, mourn together, labor and suffer together, always having before our eyes our community as members of the same body.

From that sermon came the vision that America would be a city on a hill and a light to the nations.

Second, the ideological taproot of the biblical vision entwined with the political root of the democratic ideal of the *common good.* Thomas Jefferson, an avowed deist, offered this ideal as the humanistic alternative for the biblical vision of the moral community. Realistically, however, Jefferson's democratic idea depended upon the biblical vision for its moral grounding.

Third, the biblical vision, along with the democratic ideal, combined with the economic root of the Puritan ethic. Usually referred to as the *Puritan work ethic,* which fostered industrious labor, we cannot forget that the Puritans also preached a responsible prosperity with accountability to God for the blessing of wealth. This helps explain why a *steward* means a *servant of God.*

Generally, from the 1750s to the 1850s, a revived church in an awakened nation took the lead in charitable work, from the Colonial period through the Civil War, as evidence of its stewardship. Schools, hospitals, orphanages, and missions of mercy symbolized the American response to the needs of illiterate, impoverished, sick, and lonely masses. As Nathan Hatch wrote in his book *The Democratization of American Christianity,* a revived church has always been … *remarkably effective in forging moral communities among the poor, sick, ignorant, and elderly, the most vulnerable people on earth.*[23]

This stewardship era was built on the thinking and presuppositions of thinkers who went before them, such as Martin Luther when he wrote:

> A man is generous because he trusts God and never doubts that he will always have enough. In contrast, a man is covetous and anxious because he does not trust God. Now faith is the master workman and

---

[23] Nathan Hatch, *The Democratization of American Christianity in the United States and Canada* (New Haven: Yale University Press, 1989).

the motivating force behind the good works of generosity, just as it is in all the other commandments. Without this faith, generosity is of no use at all, it is just a careless squandering of money.[24]

Revitalization in the 1740s and 1750s came through the spiritual renewal of the First Great Awakening, under the leadership of Jonathan Edwards and George Whitefield. Personal redemption fed social responsibility, and the taproot of the biblical vision of the moral community was kept alive.

Alexis de Tocqueville, the French historian, caught the spirit of Christian stewardship when he witnessed a barn-raising that engaged the energies of the whole community at work and helping one another and wrote, "America has the soul of a Church."[25] While traces of the biblical stewardship assumptions are evident today, mostly it has been replaced both in word and deed by the next period of history.

■ THE PHILANTHROPIC ERA, 1850–1950 ■

A gradual but significant shift away from the biblical stewardship worldview started in the mid-1800s, when America became more urbanized, industrialized, and capitalized. The Carnegies and Rockefellers accumulated massive fortunes and established the first foundations. They also embraced the concept of *philanthropy*, which means *friend of humankind*, as distinct from the steward, who is a servant of God. With this change in wording, God gets removed from giving. The giving process becomes secularized. In the Philanthropic era, the ideological, political, and economic roots were radically altered.

The ideological root of Social Darwinism led the way and took the place of a biblical vision for the moral community. Credit for wealth in this era was given to good fortune rather than to God. Philanthropic gifts went to the *selective good* rather than the *common good*. Professional philanthropy replaced personal stewardship and focused upon social reconstruction more than individual redemption. Rather than helping people succeed in society with charity, the focus shifted to remaking society and serving as a catalyst for political, economic, and social change.

---

[24] Martin Luther (1483–1546), "Treatise on Good Works 3," in *Selected Writings of Martin Luther: 1529–1546*, ed. Theodore Gerhardt Tappert (Minneapolis: Fortress, 1967), 191.

[25] Alexis de Tocqueville, *Democracy in America* (New York: New American Library, 1956). Originally published 1835.

The prophet for the Philanthropic period was Andrew Carnegie. In his essay entitled *The Gospel of Wealth*, he explained his own good fortune as evidence of natural selection and survival of the fittest among the human species. With one swift stroke, Carnegie cut the taproot of biblical stewardship and adopted what he called *scientific philanthropy* based upon Darwinian Theory. He attacked boldly the indiscriminate charity of Christian stewardship by saying, "It is better for mankind that the millions (of dollars) of the rich were thrown into the sea than to encourage the slothful, the drunken, the unworthy."[26]

Carnegie went another step by redefining the democratic ideal of the common good. He wrote, "The best means of benefiting the community is to place within its reach ladders upon which the aspiring can rise." With these words, he drew the line of distinction between those who were worthy of charity and those whom he judged to be unworthy of his help. The selective good replaced the root of the common good.

Severing the third root of the Puritan ethic followed naturally. In place of a responsible prosperity preached by the Puritans, Carnegie espoused an entrepreneurial ethic, putting charity on a business basis. According to him, the motive of philanthropy was not response to human suffering but calculated cost benefit for continuous economic growth with the redistribution of wealth to sustain free enterprise.

As radical and as selfish as this may seem, Carnegie recognized that his giving would be interpreted by the general public as a continuation of Christian stewardship, to which we still gave lip service. Mark Twain, however, in his 1889 black comedy called *A Connecticut Yankee in King Arthur's Court*, criticized Carnegie's motivation to use charity to benefit the industrial complex as nothing more than an instrument for enlarging the "destructive capacity of the human race."[27] When philanthropy is motivated to help only people who are a good business investment, charity becomes a form of exploitation.

This beginning of the Philanthropic period, then, cut the roots of the biblical vision in favor of Darwinian Theory, forsook the common good of the needy for the selective good of the worthy, and twisted

---

[26] Andrew Carnegie, *The Gospel of Wealth and other Timely Essays*, (Cambridge: Belknap Press of Harvard University Press, 1962).

[27] Peter Dobkin Hall, *Inventing the Nonprofit Sector*, (Baltimore, MD: Johns Hopkins University Press, 1992), p. 40.

the ethic of responsible prosperity into charity as a cost benefit. By secularizing the process of giving, the seeds of its own decay were sown.

In the midst of this shift from Stewardship to the Philanthropic period, the spiritual impulse of revival and awakening continued to influence how people used their possessions. As an outgrowth of the Second Great Awakening, led by Charles Finney in the mid-1880s, for instance, redeemed men and women founded voluntary associations across the country to meet human needs that could not be met by the church alone. The YMCA and the YWCA, followed later by the Red Cross and the United Way, are a few examples.

Even President Abraham Lincoln, despite his preoccupation with the Civil War issues, reflected on this steady erosion of values when in 1863 he called for a National Day of Humiliation when he said:

> We have grown in numbers, wealth and power, as no other nation has ever grown. But we have forgotten God.... We have vainly imagined, in the deceitfulness of our hearts, that all these blessings were produced by some superior wisdom and virtue of our own.[28]

By the end of the century, Carnegie's concept of giving based upon Social Darwinism with its elitist mentality, selective philanthropy, and economic cost benefits came under challenge by a best-selling novel by Charles Shelton entitled *In His Steps*. In the book he tells about a "dusty, worn, shabby-looking young man"[29] who stumbles into the morning worship of the reverend Henry Maxwell's wealthy downtown church. In a calm voice, he rises in the service to say, "I'm not an ordinary tramp, though I don't know of any teaching of Jesus that makes one kind of tramp less worthy from saving than another, do you?" He then explains that he is a printer by trade who lost his job to a linotype machine ten months ago. For three days now, he has tramped through their city in search of a job and a word of encouragement. Without bitterness or rancor, he asks the question, "What do you mean when you sing, 'I'll go with Him, with Him, all the way?' Do you mean that you are suffering and denying yourselves? Are you trying to save the lost and suffering humanity as I understand Jesus did?" Then he tells

---

[28] Abraham Lincoln (1809–1865) as recounted on January 31, 2007, in the *Congressional Record, V. Pt. 2* (January 18, 2007 to February 1, 2007), p. 2800.
[29] Peter Dobkin Hall, Ibid., pp. 123–125.

about his wife dying in a tenement owned by a member of the church and asks, "I wonder if following Jesus was true in his case?" With that, the tramp falls forward and dies on the communion table.

From then on, the meaning of Christian discipleship for that church is changed. Once again, discipleship means stewardship, and stewardship, means self-sacrifice for the needy, whether or not they are deemed worthy. The people of the congregation ask only one question as they confront the needs of their community: "What would Jesus do?"[30]

The problem was not in the practice of business itself—as if there is anything inherently secular in the practice of business. Francis Schaeffer wrote:

> If industrialization had been accompanied by a strong emphasis on the compassionate use of accumulated wealth and on the dignity of each individual, the industrial revolution would have indeed been a revolution for good. But all too often … the Church was silent … on a compassionate use of wealth … Following Industrialization non-compassionate use of wealth became commonplace.[31]

Time has only magnified these earlier secular tendencies. We live in a culture that worships at the shrine of four related idols: pleasure, wealth, professional status, and physical appearance. It is a culture of convenience rather than duty and of avoidance of pain rather than seeking to relieve the burdens of others. To what extent have the idols of this age—materialism, smug professionalism, and the quest for self—influenced our search for the good life above knowing God? John Wesley expressed his profound concern, "I fear riches have increased, the essence of religion has decreased in the same proportion."

The cultural drift at this point is well established, but the influence continues to play itself out today. For example, as missions grew, ministers got distracted, thinking they needed money for ministry to happen (contra Acts 1–9), and so to support that notion, they have adopted whatever methods necessary to get money. They've focused too much on worldly business and not on God's business played out in biblical stewardship.

---

[30] Charles M. Shelton, *In His Steps* (Springdale, PA: Whitaker House, 1897).
[31] Francis Schaeffer, *How Should We Then Live?: The Rise and Decline of Western Thought and Culture* (New Jersey: Fleming H. Revell Co., 1976).

THE DEVELOPMENT OR SELF-CENTERED ERA, 1950–PRESENT ◼

The continuing shift in the motives and means of using possessions was very evident around the 1950s, when fundraising became big business and development became a career. Tax law changes saw the number of foundations increase from 12,500 to over one million today, and the changes in technology to computers, the accessibility's of telephones, and the relatively inexpensive third-class mail opened the flood gates for secularized fundraising to influence how we use our possessions.

Certainly there continued to be evidence of *the moral community, the common good,* and *the ladder of opportunity,* but the *managerial motive* of the fundraising industry became the modus operandi for the development efforts. More interest was shown in research into the causes of human suffering than in the relief from that suffering. Seed grants for innovative proposals replaced sustaining grants for programs, and accounting for efficiency seemed more important than reporting for effectiveness. Business giving more and more reflected what was advantageous for the firm.

Christian organizations were quick to take on the titles, motives, and methods of secular fundraisers, doing whatever works. Many people working for Christian organizations in the 1940s and 50s held the title "stewardship representatives" and viewed their work as ministry. One example is chronicled in Robert D. Noles' book *Water Boy!,* where he talked about his "stewardship work" at Wheaton College in terms of ministry to the people he "served." He would pray each morning to see who the Lord would put on his heart and who he should visit in order to encourage them in their biblical stewardship giving![32]

In the 50s, as the Bob Noles' of Christian organizations were viewed as outdated and inefficient, they were replaced with development or advancement representatives, planned giving officers, or other names for development; their work was shifted to a *sales basis* rather than a *ministry basis.* Computer printouts started to provide their calling lists, and prayer often took a back seat. The full acceptance of the secular, philanthropy/development model was quickly the dominant force, even among Christian organizations. Fundraising became a marketing

---

[32] Robert D. Noles, *Water Boy* (Barnabas Book, 1984).

transaction, and the notion of transforming hearts in biblical steward-ship was lost, even among Christian organizations.

Mixed with this managerial motive is the political root of govern-mental involvement in regulating the means of giving by fiscal and legal statutes. Despite the fact that Ronald Reagan campaigned on the promise to restore the "biblical vision of the moral community" through voluntary agencies and George Bush championed a "thousand points of light" through individual action, the irony is that charitable orga-nizations became more and more dependent upon regulated Federal dollars during the 1980s, with further acceleration in the 1990s. As strange as it seems, up to 60 percent of today's charitable dollars comes from the Federal government, and President Clinton's era encouraged an increase in that percentage. We can understand the frustration of Robert Goheen, former President of Princeton and later President of the Council on Foundations, when he wrote, "Has charity become all law? Is it irrevocably committed to legal practitioners?"[33] If he is right, the roots of managerial motives and legally regulated means have once again redefined the meaning of giving into the process of development.

A very strong force is *identifiable self-interest.* Foundations do not hesitate to state specifically or tacitly the driving force of self-interest behind their gifts. A clear example of this shift is the ARCO founda-tion that stopped giving for the benefit of the community and shifted its giving to what benefited the business or its employees. The carry-over also affects the way in which individuals use their possessions as a reflection of our changing culture.

Perhaps this prevailing attitude accounts for the popularity of incen-tives for donors to give. Direct mail gimmicks, giving clubs, premiums, and tax benefits are used to appeal to the self-interest of the prospective giver. The practices of giving and asking for money today reflect the character values of our culture. Robert Wuthnow has written in his book *Acts of Compassion,* that our new attitude toward charitable giving "allows us to carve up our caring into little chunks that require only a level of giving that does not conflict with our needs and interests as individuals."[34] In this self-centered Development period, we volunteer

---

[33] Robert Goheen, quoted from David McKenna's "Giving is Not Guaranteed." Keynote speech to Christian Stewardship Association, September 20, 1992, Indianapolis, IN.

[34] Robert Wuthnow, *Acts of Compassion* (Princeton, NJ: Princeton University Press, 1991).

time and give money as a choice that preserves our freedom, meets our needs, and as a convenience that protects our schedules. We have almost completely separated out how we use our possessions from our spiritual life of the soul.

■ BIG GOVERNMENT AND THE DECLINE OF CHARITY ERA, PRESENT INTO THE FUTURE ■

Each of these three previously discussed aeras has paved the way for era four. The cultural shift to self-interest has been followed by a time of expanded government. Our culture is increasingly looking to the government to solve all the problems. The government has taken an increasingly significant role in the non-profit sector by viewing the tax breaks given for donations as a government subsidy. This is why charitable deductions may be done away with. Charity is now understood under the umbrella of tax law, and it is defined as such.

If history is a guide, all indications are that big government will result in moving our culture to: (1) crowd out the need for churches and (2) diminish the need for independent social service organizations. If you want to see this in action, just look to Europe. The US is only a few years behind. In a *Wall Street Journal* article, sociologist Bradford Wilcox wrote:

> A successful [big government] revolution providing cradle-to-career education and cradle-to-grave health care would reduce the odds that Americans would turn to their local religious congregations and fellow believers for economic, social, emotional and spiritual aid. Fewer American would also be likely to feel obliged to help their fellow citizens through local Churches and charities.[35]

It appears that if we accept this big government scenario, then we must also accept its byproducts of increased taxation and a loss of local or individual control of charity. Government will control the distribution of funds as necessary to assist, aid, educate, care for, or support those in need. With total coverage of need by government, charity would no longer be required, and support for charitable organizations would no longer be necessary.

---

[35] Bradford Wilcox, "God Will Provide, Unless the Government Gets There First," *Wall Street Journal*, March 13, 2009.

So there you have a ride through 270 years of American history and a peek into the future. It appears that the biblical vision of the *moral community,* the democratic ideal of the *common good,* and the Puritan ethic of *responsible prosperity* have given way to *identifiable self-interest, selective good, and self-fulfillment,* and this has opened the gate to big government. Whether or not this movement, along with an increased government involvement in charity, will change charity as we know it and dramatically limit the place of charity in the national mind remains to be seen. I believe, however, that it is important that we all open our eyes to a worldview that helps us plan our Christian life and work accordingly, lest we slowly and unwittingly become irretrievably lost.

Having digested this information, we now understand how the biblical vision of the moral community, the democratic ideal of the common good, and the Puritan ethic of responsible prosperity have given way to the motive of self-interest, the goal of the public good, and the means of self-benefit. Nowhere within the current paradigm do you find a place for the eternal soul or the God who created it.

Today, the term *stewardship* is void of all spiritual meaning. The environmentalists use the term for stewardship of the earth, and secular fundraisers refer to good stewardship as making sure a person is appropriately thanked for a gift and that the gift is used for the purpose designated by the donor.

In Robert Wuthnow's three-year study on religious and economic values, 89 percent of the respondents agreed, "Our society is much too materialistic," 74 percent said materialism is a serious social problem, and 71 percent said society would be better off if less emphasis were placed on money.[36] We see materialism in our neighbors, and we decry its presence on television or in the movies, but we do not seem to be able to find it in our own hearts. Lifestyles of those within the church vary little—if at all—from the lifestyle of others in the same income bracket.

Even more alarming is the fact that the church as a whole allows its voice to be silenced by the surrounding culture. Partially from the old fear of sounding as if all the church wants is money, and partially because of greater confusion over what the Bible really does teach

---

[36] Robert Wuthnow, "Pious Materialism: How Americans View Faith and Money," *The Christian Century,* (March 3, 1993).

about money, pastors shy away from speaking out on economic issues and their connection to core spiritual values.

In addition, secular approaches to fundraising emerged to fill the void, even in our churches. Christian stewardship—that biblical approach practiced by the Puritans—is seldom even mentioned today, let alone taught or practiced. And it is no accident that at a time when the church is fractured and culturally feeble, the values of Christian stewardship are also neglected.

Where do we go from here? Some may say, "The giving of $200 billion to charity in the United States is more than any other nation, it is going up, the largest percentage goes to religion, and whatever works is fine with me." Others may note that we are moving into a time when the largest transfer of wealth in the history of the world—as much as $100 trillion—will pass from one generation to the next. If this is true, why raise these issues?

It seems, however, that there is concern from many fronts. Robert Payton, retired President of the Center on Philanthropy, states the following in the book *The Responsibilities of Wealth*: "The strength of American giving is based upon its religious origins and values and traditions. Giving as we know it today may not survive a serious deterioration of its religious values.[37] Note that he uses the word *philanthropy* as synonymous with giving.

Jacob Riis, in his book *How the Other Half Lives*, sees philanthropy as "a bridge founded upon justice and built of human hearts."[38] Peter Dobkin Hall, a student of nonprofit organizations at Yale, then follows his words with this conclusion, "Without discovering its religious roots, American giving is unlikely to play a significant role in building such a bridge."[39] Unless we rediscover our religious roots, the distinctive American character of giving and asking for money will be lost.

The key question for the church today, according to Bellah, is "whether our organized religion can offer a genuine alternative to tendencies that are deeply destructive in our current pattern of institutions or whether religious institutions are simply one more instance of

---

[37] Robert Payton, "God and Money," In D. F. Burlingame, ed., *The Responsibilities of Wealth* (Bloomington: Indiana University Press, 1992).

[38] Jacob Riis, *How the Other Half Lives* (New York: Sagamore Press, 1957). Originally published in 1892.

[39] Peter Dobkin Hall, *Inventing the Nonprofit Sector* (Baltimore, MD: Johns Hopkins University Press, 1992), 133.

the problem."[40] As for individuals in our churches, Bellah says that the critical question is whether we are loyal to the divine mission of the church or we simply use it as an "instrument for self-fulfillment and abandon it as soon as it doesn't meet our needs."[41]

The message is clear from the secular prophets. Hear one of the prophets of God, Isaiah, speak on the issue. He draws a direct line from righteousness to justice and mercy in his prophecy to Israel. If righteousness prevails, there is justice for all people and compassion for the needy. If righteousness is lost, oppression of the week and neglect of the needy are the inevitable outcomes. Those who live in this nation, especially the church, cannot escape that truth.

Are you on the wrong trail? Have you been swallowed up by culture? Is your use of possessions tied to your soul? If so, you have a life-and-death stake in the recovery of our biblical roots. It seems clear that a moral vision for the common good by prosperous people cannot be sustained without the revitalization of our biblical stewardship roots. The First Great Awakening of the 18th century planted those roots; the Second Great Awakening of the 19th century kept those roots alive; and though they are withered in our 21st century, they are not yet dead.

The big unknown is who will make a difference? It is clear that the gospel of Jesus urges us to be at the leading edge of culture. These same gospels place in prominence how we deal with our possessions as good stewards of God's world. Even though culture has influence, it appears that there is always time for us to put God and his teaching first. Denver Seminary Distinguished Professor of New Testament Craig Blomberg, in the book *Revolution in Generosity*, raises the core issue: why is it that "Christian ministries that are raising money do not stress the central Biblical truths that giving is a part of whole-life transformation, that stewardship and sanctification go together as signs of Christian obedience and maturity, and that God will call us to account for what we do with 100 percent of the possessions He has loaned us."[42]

Despite the course history is taking, are you willing to make a difference?

---

[40] Ibid., p. 184.
[41] Ibid., p. 184.
[42] Craig Blomberg, "God and Money: A Biblical Theology of Possessions," in Wesley K. Willmer, ed., *Revolution in Generosity: Transforming Stewards to be Rich Toward God* (Chicago: Moody Publishers, 2008), 45.

Wesley K. Willmer
PH.D., CCNL

W ith over four decades of working in Christ-centered ministries, Wes Willmer is known as a thought leader among Christian organizations. Hugh O. Maclellan, Jr., has written, "Wes Willmer has been a pioneer among Christian leaders in encouraging Christians to follow God's plan for money, giving and asking." Some of Willmer's work on this topic includes *Money for Ministry, Revolution in Generosity: Transforming Stewards to be Rich Toward God, God and Your Stuff: The Vital Link Between Your Possessions and Your Soul,* and The Prospering Parachurch: Enlarging the Boundaries of God's Kingdom—a sample of his work as an author, co-author, editor, or editor-in-chief of twenty-three books and many professional journal publications. Wes has initiated and directed over $1 million in research grants to study nonprofit leadership. Board involvement includes: chair of the board of the Christian Stewardship Association, founding member of the CASE Commission on Philanthropy, the executive committee of the ECFA board (vice chair), a founding board member of the CLA, and consultant to many other organizations. Professional assignments have included working for ECFA, Biola University, Wheaton College, Roberts Wesleyan College, and Seattle Pacific University. He now serves as Executive Vice President with the Portland Oregon headquartered Mission Increase Foundation.

Willmer received a Bachelor of Arts degree in psychology and a master of education degree in counseling and guidance from Seattle Pacific University. He received a doctor of philosophy degree in higher education from the State University of New York at Buffalo. Chuck Colson wrote about the book Revolution in Generosity, "If the ideas in this book were followed, there would be a revolution in generosity among Christians."

2

ON BEING A STEWARD:
YES, IT INVOLVES MONEY

BY MARK L. VINCENT, PH.D., CCNL

The word *stewardship* gets a lot more play in our conversations than does the word *steward*.

Stewardship is now used more widely in secular speech and for secular meanings than it is to convey a spiritual mission or motivation.[43] Google the word *stewardship,* and you will find its most frequent use connects to caring for the environment. In regular conversation, *stewardship* tends to mean something that the speaker thinks is an appropriate use of a resource under his or her care and is used as a means to justify his or her choices. These are not entirely inappropriate uses of the word, but they are largely unhooked from the historic and Christian use of the word.

---

[43] See Wes Willmer's larger discussion on this in the previous chapter.

However, it is not the word *stewardship* that is central to this conversation but the word *steward*.[44] In the Scriptures, the word *steward* is a title given to the Christian and names the role the Christian is to play.

> Question: what is the steward's role?
> Answer: *a Christian is a steward of the gospel.*[45]

The gospel for which the Christian is a steward is the good news that God forgives sin and made possible a restored relationship with God, self, others, and creation by the gift of God in Jesus Christ.

This gospel is cared for through two key actions: 1) obedience to the Great Commission by inviting others to accept the forgiveness God offers and 2) living the Great Commandment to love God with all one's heart, soul, mind, and strength and to love neighbor as self.[46]

Stewards of the gospel do these things because stewards believe that if they do not, then what they compete against will win. And the steward competes against what would lay hold of and destroy others: warmongering, slavery, famine, natural disaster, unchecked greed, environmental devastation, hatred of self, bigotry, family and societal destruction, oppression, addiction, and disease. These are a few of the steward's hideous competitors.

---

[44] The following definition is used in *A Stewardship Manifest*, an e-book available from Design Group International:

> A steward is a special kind of servant. She or he is trusted to take care of someone else's assets. These assets can be property, equipment, wealth, or even people. The steward is a servant who treats their charge as if it were their own.
> Stewardship is the act of willingly and responsibly caring for this charge.
> Being a steward and carrying out stewardship rests on several assumptions:
> - That I hold a charge (something to take care of) from someone or something that requires my service.
> - That my highest level of personal fulfillment and most significant life achievement is found in accepting this charge.
> - That I am not an individual living alone. I have a connection to the rest of the human community, and to the rest of creation, which benefits from the way I take care of my charge.
> - That I willingly accept this service.

[45] 1 Corinthians 4:1; 1 Peter 4:10, 11

[46] In the Good Samaritan parable, Jesus defines a neighbor as one's enemy, even the person against whom one is deeply prejudiced, certainly the one who has been harmed and ignored by others.

Money, time, talent, one's network of relationships, a person's body, one's spirituality, one's vocation, access to creation's natural endowments, any leadership role a person may play in an organization or society, and any other gift attributed to God's handiwork are tools for the life of a person pledged to be a steward of the gospel in the face of the hideous competition.

Money, in particular, is a most potent and powerful tool for the life of the steward. Money must be wrestled into place as a servant of the Master, or it becomes the master we serve. When money becomes the master, our hideous competitors win.

Jesus Christ, whom all little Christs follow, tells us money has a god-like power.[47] A good deal of my work since 1995 has been developing and passing along an understanding of how this is so. This chapter summarizes that work, describes how well we are doing in our wrestling match with money, and offers inspiration for all steward leaders to renew their commitment to keep wrestling.

Money has a god-like power because:[48]

1. **Money outlives you.** It was here before you got here and will pass from you to others once you are gone.

2. **Money has a greater circle of influence than you do**. It goes places you cannot go and fosters accomplishments beyond your capacity. Possessing money grants a person increased capacity to go and accomplish. Money provides possibility.

3. **Money is mysterious.** Its qualities and capacities cannot be fully known. Economic models are nothing more than weather forecasting, with ever more refined guesses exposing just how much more we do not yet know about the dynamics of money. Financial advisors and economic advisors can only postulate. They fastidiously avoid pronouncements. They fail even more spectacularly than they succeed.

---

[47] Matthew 6:24.

[48] Detailed in the book *A Christian View of Money: Celebrating God's generosity* (3rd ed), Wipf and Stock, 2005, by Mark L. Vincent.

4. **Money dwells in the realm of what we are tempted to worship.** Humans worship what they believe to be eternal, powerful, and mysterious—essentially, the first three items on this list.

   Most of western culture has ceased the worship of natural forces or government leaders or fertility because although we may be in subjection to them, we think we know how they work. They are deities to us no longer, and they no longer live in the realm of what we worship. We might not sacrifice children to make hurricanes go away, but we still sacrifice the well-being of children in pursuit of wealth. We do not pray to the fertility gods anymore, but we spend gargantuan amounts of money for sexual-performance-enhancing drugs. We no longer have a death cult, but we want the lowest possible health insurance premiums, even if it means shutting others with preexisting conditions out of the benefit pool.

   Money still lives in this realm of what we worship. We are sorely tempted to offer ourselves to it, whether we possess money or not. Far too many pledge their lives to money; sacrifice spouses, children, or personal integrity to possess it; or place themselves in thrall to their next paycheck because they spent what they have not yet earned.

5. **Money mimics everything God promises in the New Jerusalem.** The descriptions of the city and society God builds[49] are full of references to economic sufficiency, meaningful existence, and personal well-being. The difference between God's promised new society and the pull of money in today's society is that we wait for the promise of God's eternal benefits, while money provides a right-now fix. Consider these three examples:

   - Why hope for a mansion in heaven when I can buy/build the house of my dreams with enough money?
   - What benefit is there in waiting for a resurrection body when enough money buys the cosmetics and body sculpting to have that body now?
   - Why pray to God for the health of my child when money pays for the prescription she needs?

---

[49] See Isaiah 65 and Revelation 19–21.

When money is plentiful, one's hope is too easily rooted in the here and now rather than in aspirations for future generations or life eternal. Another way to say this is *we pray for what we cannot pay for.*

6. **Money is an instrument we wield.** Money is a sharp-bladed instrument, destroying or healing, often doing both with the same stroke.

   Consider the image of a scalpel or a soldier's bayonet. Both bring destruction. Both hold the hope of making a better way in the future. When they are employed, the outcome is unknown. More often than not, trauma and healing get linked with no capacity to separate them. This is one way we know we live in a fallen world. Evil has adhered itself to the good.

   Money's capacity to simultaneously bless and curse means the good we hope to accomplish for ourselves, our families, our vocations, and even for our congregations, is rife with ripples of harm we cannot always see. Whether we use money or refrain from using it, we cannot avoid living in the economic realm, having impact upon it, or having an inability to control the outcomes. Each dollar we spend or save quivers with the potential to bring joy or grief. More often than not, both happen at the same time, in spite of our intent.

   I write this as the husband of a sixteen-time cancer survivor.[50] Over the past twelve years, we learned to rejoice when we had enough money to cover medical bills, even though spending money for treatment means not having money to save, to share, or to enjoy. We also know every dollar spent on Lorie's care is not available in that moment for someone else's care who needs it and who may be sicker than Lorie. Joy and sorrow are deeply intertwined in this life. Wielding money brings both.

7. **Everything can be monetized.** Whatever it is you want to do, even the most altruistic desire, gets a price tag placed on it. We create marketplaces for everything, from carbon emissions, to sewage cleanup, to cyberspace. Participation in an economy is

---

[50] This story is told in the book *Fighting Disease, Not Death: Finding a Way through Lifelong Struggle*, Design Group International, 2011, by Mark and Lorie Vincent.

inescapable. It is as pervasive in our lives as God intends it to be.

8. **Money can influence you to think you are God.** Having access to money helps us purchase technology, making it possible to be virtually present in several simultaneous locations, increasing our access to knowledge and broadening our sovereignty over the little universes we think we create. Omnipresence, omniscience, and sovereignty are qualities we would normally assign to Deity, but with money, we approximate them now and start believing that divine pretending is our birthright.

9. **Money transforms life.** Do you have a lot of money? Remove it, and watch how pervasive the resulting changes are. Do you have few funds? Notice how profoundly life changes when there is sudden access to wealth. The transformational change in either direction shows yet again how money is an instrument of simultaneous pain and gain. Worry and benefit are found at both ends of economic life, shaping how one sees him or herself, how one lives in relationship to others, and what one's values are.

For all these reasons, and reasons not yet discovered, money is akin to a god.

This mystery that is money—this god-like entity that competes with God for our affections and power we must wrestle to the ground else it becomes our master—touches all the other tools a steward uses, potentially confusing a person into thinking that those tools are the most precious elements they care for, instead of the gospel. A person can be tempted to view these endowments as a material trust to accomplish a solely material goal rather than a material trust for an eternal purpose.

Yes, many would say Christians believe they are stewards of the endowments God gives—endowments such as money, time, talents, and so on. No argument against this point of view can be found here. Instead, the invitation of this chapter is to expand our understanding of the purposes of these endowments. When viewed through the lens of

Christian faith, these endowments become tools for the gospel, not an end in themselves. They become purposed for the Great Commission and the Great Commandment.

One way to understand this is the old Irish tradition of the High King.[51] Such a king is believed to be king of all kings. Lesser kings have subjects and domains, but in the presence of the High King, they bow the knee and give tribute and allegiance. Similarly, we have many endowments from God, but the High King of Endowments is the gospel. All other endowments are pressed into its service as tools for its domain.

As we move to consider our performance in this wrestling match with money, let's remember that the gospel is the proclamation that God chooses not to hold our sins against us and that all creation's relationship with God can be restored because of the work of Jesus Christ. Christians believe this gospel is the pearl of great price[52] and places everything they have and are in service to it, including money.

We 21st century western culture Christians have moved far from this understanding. Some of the strongest indictments of how far we've moved are found in the annual reports of the state of giving available from Empty Tomb, Inc.[53] Wes Willmer's opening chapter in this book provides the historical overview of this decline in faith and practice. In addition, a recent eye-opening description comes from William F. High in *Christian Research Journal*,[54] in an article titled "Short-term Recession or the Long Winter." He demonstrates how Christians moved away from teaching that God is the owner of all to teaching that God is the recipient of a percentage, to teaching that it is good to give a ministry a little something so that it can keep going. Mr. High then calls for Christians—if that is what they truly are—to return to the original and correct understanding of God as owner.

In the move from God is the owner of all to God is the recipient of a percentage, we do not just shift downward in the amount of the gift. We also stop considering how to give from all our assets to thinking only about giving gifts from our take-home income. We also attempt

---

[51] http://www.historyfiles.co.uk/KingListsBritain/GaelsHighKings.htm. Retrieved 21 December 2011.

[52] Matthew 13:45, 46.

[53] www.emptytomb.org

[54] (33:1, 32–38)

to change God's role from an owner who entrusts us with our endowments to a recipient of tribute we bring from what *we* own.

In the next downward move from God as the recipient of our tithes to ministries hoping to persuade us that they are worth any gift we choose to give, we do not just ratchet down our giving even more; we also choose to center giving around human activity rather than a worshipful response to divine grace. Even more, we ignore and cease to properly support the local fellowship of believers as the cell structure of Christ's body, creating long-term damage in our capacity to take good care of the gospel and our ability to teach about the life of the steward.[55]

It is a long way back, and it starts with my declaring myself a steward of the gospel, bringing all of life's resources to bear on this precious gift I've been given as a trust. It then proceeds to you joining me, consecrating not just your income and estate to the Lord, but also the way in which you earn them, the way you organize your time, the methods by which you gain wisdom and how you dispense it, in how you develop and influence your social networks, and by how you live within God's creation.

From here, it moves outward to others as we say and show what it means to be forgiven and reconciled to God, inviting others to join us in our battle against the hideous competition.

It moves further outward still as we function as steward leaders in the places and organizations where God sends us[56] and in how we participate in the economy with our incomes and estates.[57]

Have you lost touch with your life as a steward? Have the tools of the steward become replacement gods you now serve?

Wrestle the money demi-god to the ground. Free yourself from its shackles, and begin again. Pray the prayer, *God be merciful to me, a sinner.* Sing the hymn "I Surrender All." And as you do, let the wonder and awe of God's forgiveness renew your desire to take good care of the gospel message—for the glory of God rather than for your material gain, personal tribute, or organizational advancement.

Be free that others may know freedom.

---

[55] For more on this subject, see the chapter written by Leslie and Natalie Francisco.
[56] The chapters written by Scott Rodin, Gary Hoag, and Rebecca Basinger provide an even deeper discussion on this subject.
[57] See Gary Moore's chapter for more on this theme.

But once this commitment to live free as a steward of the gospel is in place, how is it cultivated all lifelong? Even more, how is it cultivated in others so that they too will want to cultivate it in those who come after them? Here is a passage adapted from *A Stewardship Manifest*, a resource I originally wrote at the request of Mennonite Mutual Aid (now renamed as Everence), that attempts to answer the question:

There are three essential elements:

1. **Experience**
2. **Storytelling**
3. **Practice**

Experience: Linking the word *experience* with the life of the steward tempts people to think the first step is cultivating an experience with giving. Not so. Experiencing God's grace while giving is a good thing, but we are after something far more profound here—something even more fundamental to the development process. *That is an experience in receiving God's grace.*

Christians come into the kingdom in a receiving posture, after all. We become Christians by admitting our need for God's grace. It is in receiving this grace that we find grace to give to others.

The exodus story of the Hebrew people is helpful in thinking about this. It is so full of God's gracious intervention that it drips all over whoever hears it. A people enslaved and oppressed find their freedom through God's actions. God punishes their oppressor without violence on the Hebrew's part. The plagues and the Red Sea rescue and then the feeding in the desert become permanent reminders of God's gracious care.

The Hebrews experienced a generous God. They received God's grace. When you hear the story, you are invited to enter into the same kind of relationship with God. And once you are in touch with God as a sustaining source of grace, you become better equipped to live a generous life.

Storytelling: Telling this story of meeting God's grace, and your response to it, is important. Telling the story reminds you of your new identity as one who received God's grace. Telling the story invites others into an experience with God's grace.

Storytelling is a form of worshiping God. Telling the story keeps you aware of God's continuing activity in your life and the lives of others and gives you opportunity to express your thanks to God. You remain more deeply grounded in your faith. You draw more deeply on God's grace in the past as a source of strength for tomorrow.

Practice: Practice is following through on what your grace experience teaches you. As you tell the story and are in touch with God's grace to you, opportunities to respond jump out at you—how you treat snippy store clerks, how you tip city cab drivers, how you respond to those who offend you. Practice is acting on those opportunities.

Practice can take at least three forms:

- The practice of giving and distributing through acts of worship;
- The practice of love through acts of serving;
- The practice of saying "thank you" to family, friends, neighbors, and strangers.

The exodus story is helpful once more when considering stewardship practice. The Hebrew people gave in acts of worship. They had the tradition of the burnt offering,[58] and they had a tradition of all gifts being consecrated for God's use. In addition, they were involved in distribution of these gifts. For instance, they knew their gifts would be used in the tabernacle construction of Exodus 35. Their giving of burnt offerings in Leviticus 1 meant they knew the entire gift would be consumed in worship to God. They knew when giving a grain offering that a portion would be given to priests and their families.[59] And they knew their first fruits gifts would be partly offered in worship, partly used for a family feast at God's house, and partly given to others for their use.[60] There were not to be surprise diversions of contributed wealth under some form of priestly authority. Rather, the priestly community was to carry out the purpose of the gift.

Practice is also love in action. Graciousness and hospitality are shown to the stranger and the alien. Charity is given to the widow and the orphan. The sick and imprisoned are visited. Strong relationships of

---

[58] Leviticus 1.
[59] Leviticus 2.
[60] Deuteronomy 14.

mutual aid are cultivated within the worshiping community. Spouses are treated with deepest respect. Children are granted time, attention, discipline, and material provision. Lives are ordered with a balance of work, Sabbath, play, and worship so that one is strong and available for these acts of service. Proper rest, diet, and exercise are sought so a gracious and hospitable outlook can be maintained.

Learning becomes a worshipful act of using the mind. Labor becomes an act of gratitude to the God, who designed the human body and gave us the intellect to solve problems. Care for the earth becomes worship of the Creator. Participation in civic affairs becomes an act of thanksgiving to God, who gives us the human community. Commitment to one's friends is a way of celebrating God's merciful friendship with us. Monetary investment becomes a prayer to improve living conditions, peace, and prosperity for all people. The distribution of assets we accumulate during our lifetime becomes an opportunity to sing God's praises.

■ THE CYCLE BEGINS AGAIN ■

As we live the worshipful life of the steward, as we take the risks, it becomes clear we cannot do it by ourselves. Money, time, and talent are too complicated to handle in a purified state, especially with all the evil around us. People will twist our words, misperceive our intent, and judge us in spite of our best wishes. Money gets misdirected or siphoned off. Those who supervise our work don't always understand our commitments, or sometimes, they waste our time. Our neighbor's lifestyle might undo all the environmental stewardship we practice. So in this worshipful practice of being a steward, we find we must plead for the grace of God again and again. And as we do, God meets us with

All three of these bleed together—experience, storytelling, and practice. If you experience God's grace, you will have a story to tell, and you will act in a different way. As you live out your experience with God's grace, you get in touch with grace all over again, giving you a new story to tell and new activity that, once again, touches you with the grace of God, giving you a story to tell and inviting you to respond, which connects you with God's grace and gives you a story to tell and …

his grace. We learn all over again that God makes up the difference between our intent and the results he seeks.

Each time we come in contact with God's grace, the *experience* gives us a new *story* to tell. As we tell it, new *practices* of worship and service become clear. And as we live out the worship and service, we discover yet again our need for God's grace. Seeking grace and finding it gives us a new *experience,* a new *story* to tell, and a new challenge to *practice* our faith. The cycle goes on and on.

So a lifelong life of the steward that teaches others to be stewards all lifelong in such a way that they develop still other lifelong stewards involves these three things: experience, story, and practice. The problem is our long-standing effort to cut the heart out of all three.

- ***We foster independence rather than interdependence.*** We deceive ourselves into thinking we can find completeness under our own efforts. We think we arrive when we no longer need anyone. This mentality produces an inability to receive the grace of God modeled in things like covenant marriage, neighbors who keep an eye on each others' property, or handshakes that guarantee as much follow through as a business contract—let alone God's concern for us. We end up with fewer needs we can safely admit and fewer venues in which to admit them. This erases the possibility of an experience with grace.

- ***We expect and enforce silence.*** We say, ***"Don't let the left hand know what the right hand is doing,"*** to enforce this silence, not realizing this quote from Jesus[61] is a reference to almsgiving, not worship. When we use these words to enforce silence, we forget that giving is to be a public declaration of God's sovereignty. When the public declaration is shut off, no stories get told, and no one else hears the invitation to experience God's grace.

- ***We set up an elite, usually older, cadre of people at the heart of the worshiping community.*** This cadre does most of the giving and decides where most of the money goes. This deflates the joy of collecting and distributing funds for ministry to all others, for who enjoys giving to something that does not

[61] Matthew 6:3.

involve all of who they are and have? Who is invited beyond obligation, philanthropy, or prosperity thinking toward the worshipful life of the steward when decision-making power has been removed? How can I engage in this practice of worshiping God and loving others through my service if I am merely funding the service of others?

Do we really want deeper experiences with God's grace? Then we need to lead people in getting in touch with their money stories—so that the money god is wrestled to the ground from the beginning of their experiences in the economy. And we need to build this activity into new member preparation and pre-marital counseling so that as new households come into God's household, they know that God is God and money is not.

Do we want to tell the stories of God's grace? Then we must tell these stories to our children, the children in our homes, the children in our churches, and the children of the faith who find Christ as adults.

Do we want more practice in place? Then a congregation's own story of life as a steward of the gospel needs to be fostered. How is money used in support of the congregation's mission so that God's grace is displayed and new stories are discovered that can be told to yet another generation of generous Christians? We must visibly make the connections between congregational giving and distributions so that households are challenged to do the same with their income and spending.

Christians are stewards of the gospel.

Money both threatens that stewardship and makes it possible.

Money needs to be wrestled into place so we can live the life of the steward and compete effectively against the hideous competition.

We keep it in place by telling and retelling our experiences with God's grace and thereby discover how we can live the life of the steward more effectively.

We tell and retell these stories in the context of congregation and family so that others can learn of God's grace and respond to it by picking up the life of the steward.

Let's find our way back to this worshipful rhythm of life.

Mark L. Vincent
PH.D., CCNL

M ark L. Vincent is a lifelong student and practitioner of leadership, organizational design and development, the intersections of faith and money, and group process and problem solving. He writes, trains, and speaks broadly on these themes.

Mark is CEO and a Senior Design Partner of Design Group International, a firm established to help organizations and their leaders discover clarity and implement solutions. He works with businesses, nonprofits, and ministry organizations in untying organizational knots and moving forward in mission.

Mark's expertise in the arena of associational and denominational systems helps religious and non-profit organizations discover new ways to sustain and expand their efforts across their many chapters, congregations, and institutions. This expertise was gathered through his years in executive leadership, leadership development, pastoral ministry, academic pursuits, and more than twenty years in organizational development consulting.

Author of such books as *A Christian View of Money, Speaking About Money: Reducing the Tension,* and *Money Mania,* Mark was the founding editor of *Giving,* the annual periodical of the Ecumenical Stewardship Center. He serves on the board of Engineered Pump Services, Inc. and the Christian Leadership Alliance, regularly instructing at its annual Nonprofit Leadership Academy and teaching executive leadership for its CCNL program.

Mark is married to Lorie, a sixteen-time cancer survivor. Together, they wrote *Fighting Disease, Not Death: Finding a way through lifelong struggle.* They call Wisconsin home, but they divide their time among family in several locations.

3

PREACHING AND TEACHING THE LIFE OF THE STEWARD

BY BISHOP L. W. III AND DR. NATALIE A. FRANCISCO

S tewardship is often defined as everything we do after we say, "I believe." It encompasses how we conduct ourselves in the management of our internal and external resources as well as the daily affairs of our lives. Pastors have the responsibility of teaching our congregations that we and all that we possess belong to God. Psalm 24:1 (KJV) says, "The earth is the Lord's, and the fulness thereof; the world, and they that dwell therein." God has given us natural and acquired resources so that we can be channels of blessing to expand God's kingdom in the world.

A channel for us is our privilege to serve as senior pastors of Calvary Community Church (also known as C3) in Hampton, VA. We take this stewardship responsibility seriously, realizing that the congregants and visitors are entrusted to us by God each time they attend a worship service, event, or activity in which opportunities abound to teach, preach, and demonstrate biblical principles necessary for the spiritual growth and development of the local and universal church.

■ WHAT SHOULD WE GIVE? ■

Winston Churchill said, "We make a living by what we get; we make a life by what we give." Giving of our time, talents, and treasures to serve God should be taught and modeled by pastors in the pulpit as well as by parishioners in the pew. In so doing, we encourage and empower ourselves and the church to become good stewards of the manifold grace and gifts of God[62] given to us for the purpose of glorifying God and edifying others.

The Message Bible translation of Romans 12:1 states, "So here's what I want you to do, God helping you: Take your everyday, ordinary life—your sleeping, eating, going-to-work, and walking-around life—and place it before God as an offering. Embracing what God does for you is the best thing you can do for Him." The investment of our time, talents, and treasures at home, at work, and/or at church will yield dividends in terms of quality of life, quantity of money and other resources, and a harvest of transformed lives. This has held true in our experiences as senior pastors. Our congregation has recited Romans 12:1 as a precursor to every message we've preached and taught on Sunday mornings for years, and we have seen the benefit of giving our lives and resources to God as an offering manifest in our personal lives as well as in the lives of C3 members.

We have learned that the more we give of our time, talents, and treasures to God and others, the more we receive in return. As we continue to give the best of ourselves in abundant supply, our inner and outer resources receive constant replenishment. This is good news and proves that the principle of *Sowing and Reaping*, also referred to as *The Law of Reciprocity*, really does work. This may not make sense to some, but the Bible, which has been tested throughout the ages and found to be true, supersedes our own thoughts. God is honored and others are blessed through our giving, and one of the added benefits is that we reap a harvest of eternal weight in return.

■ WHY SHOULD WE GIVE? ■

God loves and is praised with our giving. The *Amplified* translation of 2 Corinthians 9:6–7, 10–11 declares, "[Remember] this: he who sows sparingly and grudgingly will also reap sparingly and grudgingly, and he who sows generously [that blessings may come to someone] will also reap generously and with blessings. Let each one [give] as he has made up his own mind and purposed in his heart, not reluctantly or sorrowfully or under compulsion, for God loves (He takes pleasure in, prizes above other things, and is unwilling to abandon or to do without)

---

[62] 1 Peter 4:10.

a cheerful (joyous, "prompt to do it") giver [whose heart is in his giving] … And [God] Who provides seed for the sower and bread for eating will also provide and multiply your [resources for] sowing and increase the fruits of your righteousness [which manifests itself in active goodness, kindness, and charity], wealthy in every way, so that you can be generous in every way, producing with us great praise to God."

Giving not only honors God, but also it advances the work of ministry. There is a biblical system of giving addressed in the Old and New Testaments that, when taught, adds value to the giver as well as to the overall local and global mission of the church. Practicing these principles puts everyone, regardless of economic status or background, on the same level. It is an equitable system that supports the Great Commission[63] and the Great Commandment[64] in tangible ways by integrating our faith with our finances. Tithing, which represents giving 10 percent of our increase (or income) to God, is the funding system that undergirds and perpetuates the work of ministry. Without this funding system, there are no disciples, no congregations, and no works of ministry sponsored by congregations, denominations, or parachurch organizations.[65]

We have not only taught the biblical system of giving shared in this chapter to our congregation—a sermon series that we intentionally teach from time to time as revelation to some and a refresher course to others—but also we serve as first partakers ourselves. As pastors, we consider ourselves to be practitioners of what we preach. We also require that all leaders within our ministry tithe before they are appointed to any position of leadership, and we rely on their honesty as they complete and submit their ministry candidate questionnaire to our executive administrative council. It is our belief that we can only ask or expect members to do what we as pastors and ministry leaders are doing.

We have numerous personal stories that prove God's system of giving works, regardless of the economic disparity between so-called *haves* and *have nots*—and we have lived in both camps. We, and others within our congregation, have testimonies to tell from our journeys of faith in the wilderness to financial fitness and wealth.

---

[63] Matthew 28:19–20.

[64] Matthew 22:36–40.

[65] See Wes Willmer's chapter to learn how much this system of funding has deteriorated.

Psalm 66:12 says, "You let men ride over our heads; we went through fire and water, but you brought us to a place of abundance." The KJV identifies this place of abundance as a wealthy place. The Hebrew word for wealthy is *revayah,* meaning saturation or run over. We came through the wilderness before and during our early years in ministry. At that time, we were like the children of Israel in the wilderness. At this time in our lives, it is as if we now camp in God's Promised Land! Following is just a snippet of both ends of the spectrum for us.

Our Wilderness Journey: Shortly after we were married in 1983, we filed bankruptcy because of business dealings that had gone badly with Francisco Construction company. We owed numerous creditors, including the IRS; received so many judgments/warrants in our first year of marriage that the sheriff knew us on a first-name basis; had no health or life insurance, hardly any money in our checking account, and absolutely no savings; bought our first used mattress with stains that would not come out; moved from a parents' home after being married to a one bedroom apartment that was so small that we had to get on top of our bed to make it up, put the Christmas tree in the closet, and place our daughter Nicole's crib in the living room.

In the midst of adjusting to our first year of marriage and our first child being born in 1984, we were asked to serve in interim leadership in 1985 at Calvary Mennonite Church in Newport News, VA. In 1986, the Virginia Mennonite Conference ordained Leslie into the ministry, and we accepted our call to the pastorate—a new assignment that compelled us to release Francisco Construction Company in order to obey God's call to enter full-time ministry in October of 1990, without full or part-time pay!

Our Wealthy Journey: Our faith in God and the discipline and determination to be good stewards of the resources that came into our hands by following God's giving plan led us to a wealthy place. We prayed and confessed God's Word over the vision we had for our personal lives and ministry as well as our finances, and we began to position ourselves to tithe and give offerings consistently. As a result of our continuing to tithe in the midst of our wilderness experience, God honored and stretched what little we had. Whenever there was a need, God made sure that it was met—from our needing a new pair of shoes for our firstborn child to needing a home. In the midst of what seemed like a famine after filing bankruptcy, having no substantial savings account or health or life insurance at the time, our faith and obedience caused God to perform the miraculous by allowing water to appear in a desert.[66]

Our small Newport News congregation of committed tithing members soon was able to purchase a lot in Hampton, where Calvary Community Church would be built and established as a new church plant. And that's not all—God provided everything we needed in order to construct our first home from the ground up, utilizing free labor from some of our business associates and family on a divided parcel of the same lot where the church was built.

We now serve as Senior Pastors of Calvary Community Church in Hampton, VA, and President and Executive Vice President of Calvary Covenant Ministries, Inc., which gives spiritual and administrative oversight to churches in Virginia, North Carolina, Texas, and South Africa. We founded Calvary Christian Academy, L. W. Francisco Ministries, and Women of Worth & Worship, LLC. We've also been privileged to write several books.[67] We secured key man life insurance policies for each of us so that Calvary Community Church will continue with more-than-adequate funding after our deaths; full health, dental, and life insurance coverage; mutual funds, retirement accounts, and diversified investments; an estate plan, which includes a will, medical directives, and a trust so that our assets are left as a legacy to our children and future generations, as well as to our charities of choice.

Finally, because we have been good stewards of our resources, we are able to bless other people with resources. The more we give, the more God gives back to us in ways too numerous to name!

We teach the following Principles of Tithing to our C3 congregation and other churches:

1. ***Who should give to the church? Everyone!*** First Corinthians 16:1–2 (KJV) says, "Now concerning the collection of the saints, as I have given order to the Churches of Galatia, even so do ye. Upon the first day of the week let every one of you

---

[66] Isaiah 43:19.

[67] Available from www.calvarycommunity.org, www.lwfrancisco.com, and www.nataliefrancisco.com.

lay by him in store, as God hath prospered him, that there be no gatherings when I come." This system does not discriminate based on how much one has or earns.

2. ***Non-tithers, especially non-tithing ministry leaders, are compared to thieves.*** Malachi 3:8–9 (KJV) says, "Will a man rob God? Yet you have robbed me. But ye say, Wherein have we robbed thee? In tithes and offerings. Ye are cursed with a curse: for ye have robbed me, even this whole nation." A person who steals from God has a spirit of thievery associated with him/her!

3. ***The tithe is holy and belongs to God.*** Proverbs 3:9 (KJV) says, "Honor the Lord with thy substance, and with the first fruits of all thine increase." Leviticus 27:30–31 KJV says, "And all the tithe of the land, whether of the seed of the land, or of the fruit of the tree, is the LORD's: it is holy unto the LORD. And if a man will at all redeem ought of his tithes, he shall add thereto the fifth part thereof." You might be interested to know that *The Message* Bible translates the fifth part as 20 percent!

4. ***We tithe at the local church where we worship God and are spiritually nourished.*** Malachi 3:10 (MSG) says, "Bring your full tithe to the Temple treasury so there will be ample provisions in my Temple. Test me in this and see if I don't open up heaven itself to you and pour out blessings beyond your wildest dreams." Matthew 6:21 (KJV) says, "For where your treasure is, there will your heart be also." Tithing is an expression of our commitment to God.

Once we give, we must release what we have given without feeling anxious, worried, or guilty. When we give to God, our heavenly bank account is credited immediately.[68] God honors our obedience as we give with no strings, just as God gives to us.[69] Those who abuse God's system of tithing should know that God will not overlook it!

---

[68] This is the principle of *Tzedakah,* which was in place from the beginning of ancient Judaism—the idea that God blesses those who live in the rhythm of giving charitably, adding to the impact of the gift for the recipient and the giver.
[69] James 1:5.

Tithe to worship and honor God. Some people tithe thinking they will receive finances in return, but that is not to be the motive for giving, nor is it the only reason for tithing. Tithing is the system that allows actions to back up or fortify our words by demonstrating our reverence and respect for God and His Word. Deuteronomy 14:22–23 (KJV) says, "Thou shalt truly tithe all the increase of thy seed, that the field bringeth forth year by year. And thou shalt eat before the LORD thy God, in the place which he shall choose to place his name there, the tithe of thy corn, of thy wine, and of thine oil, and the firstlings of thy herds and of thy flocks; that thou mayest learn to fear the LORD thy God always." Psalms 37:25 (KJV) says, "I have been young, and now am old; yet have I not seen the righteous forsaken, nor his seed begging bread."

We can expect angels to operate on our behalf when we tithe. Tithing prevents evil forces from wreaking havoc and destruction in our lives because angels are released to operate for our good. Psalms 104:4 (KJV) says, "Who maketh his angels spirits; his ministers a flaming fire." Matthew 18:10 (KJV) says, "Take heed that ye despise not one of these little ones; for I say unto you, That in heaven their angels do always behold the face of my Father which is in heaven."

Many may argue that tithing is an Old Testament commandment given under the law, and therefore, since we now live under the New Covenant dispensation of grace that it is not applicable for today. We disagree with this theology because the principles of tithing are clearly demonstrated in the New Testament in the behavior of the early church,[70] according to Paul's teachings,[71] and in the lives of our congregational members, including ours, and prove that God's system of giving yields benefits.

Consider these seven benefits of tithing[72]:

1. **God's house is fully supplied.** As a result of the faithful giving of our C3 congregation, we have been able to employ over sixty full and part-time staff for the past twenty-one years,

---

[70] Acts 4:32–37 and Acts 6. A close study of these passages demonstrates that the system of tithing and firstfruits and their distributions did not diminish in the early church.

[71] i.e., 1 Corinthians 16:2.

[72] Based on Malachi 3:8–12.

keep the ministry and its community and global missions programs operating effectively and efficiently, fully fund and build a C3 Habitat for Humanity House, grant benevolent funds to members in need, and give charitable contributions to other non-profit entities in our community and abroad. Over 70 percent of our members tithe. This, according to national statistics, is virtually unheard of.

2. **Opportunity and divine favor are extended to the giver.** We receive what we call *praise reports* from many members who attribute their employment and purchase of new homes and cars that were desperately needed to the fact these opportunities did not come their way until after they were committed to the principle of tithing. In fact, there were four specific instances when members were given cars that were paid for and donated to them by others in our congregation. In each case, both the givers and the receivers credited their ability to give and receive to God's favor released to them because of their consistency in giving.

3. **The devourer is rebuked and the deterioration process is halted.** The devourer, also known as Satan or the enemy of our souls, has a modus operandi to steal, kill, and destroy, according to John 10:10. However, because of the promise found not only in Malachi 3:11 but also in the latter portion of John 10:10, the devourer is rebuked as a result of our giving, which lines up with the act of the ultimate giver, Jesus Christ, who gave Himself to be the sacrifice for our sins and was resurrected so that we could live abundantly.

   When we accept the sacrifice of Jesus and the power of His resurrection and commit to showing our love and reverence by giving of our resources to expand God's kingdom, then even the resources that we have are multiplied. For example, one of our cars is fourteen years old, and it is still in good condition both physically and mechanically. The tires last longer, and there have been no major repairs to date. The deterioration process has definitely been halted!

4. **Our harvest won't spoil, and our finances will have lasting value.** Many of the scriptures shared in the Old and New Testament were shared within an agrarian culture. Although those who still work the land as farmers may be able to attest to the fact that their harvests have been blessed, others of us who live in urban areas have harvests of other kinds that are contingent upon where we work and what we do. The point is that giving to God causes the work of our hands to be blessed, and every resource, including our finances, will have long-term value.

   For example, one particular couple in our congregation shared a testimony of how their home business yielded government contracts that caused finances to be increased in the form of multiple income streams from national and international sources, which they proclaimed would not have occurred if they did not have a heart to give to God's kingdom and to bless other people. They have been featured in our local newspaper and have an incredible story of their own to share regarding their journey from wilderness to wealth that fuels even greater levels of giving.

5. **We will never be out of season (or a day late and a dollar short).** Giving allows us to position ourselves to be used by God as our faith is tested and our purpose is revealed. Dreams and visions that are planted as seeds within our hearts are birthed in the right season as a result of our giving our time, talents, and treasures in order to fulfill them. As we do our part, as we both have learned through experience, God will definitely ensure that our efforts are not in vain.[73]

6. **All nations (people) shall call us blessed.** There are many who have made statements to us and other givers within our congregation such as, "You're just lucky." "Life must have been easy for you." Well, only those who do not fully know or comprehend the story behind the glory would make such erroneous comments. Luck has nothing to do with the state of

---

[73] 1 Corinthians 15:58.

being blessed. We are blessed because we have a mind and heart to give as an expression of our love and obedience to God. Other people, whether believers or nonbelievers, will be able to see the blessing of the Lord upon us, and it is up to us to share why.

7. **We will be delightsome and valuable people.** Have you ever noticed that people enjoy being around those who are cheerful givers? It is true that God loves a cheerful giver,[74] and so do others who cross our paths. When we willingly give the best of who we are and what we have to honor God and encourage those around us, we add value to the world around us and serve as delightsome company.

The Bible clearly teaches and therefore endorses God's system of giving. We serve Him and others by properly managing our time, talents (natural gifts and developed skills), and treasures. Pastors and ministers of the gospel are not exempt from serving as examples of good stewardship and teaching those who attend our churches to do the same. Some shy away from the subject of stewardship altogether, especially when it involves the management of money. However, money is a valuable resource that is necessary to advance the mission of the church beyond its walls and into the community, across the nation, and around the globe.

When our faith is interwoven into the fabric of our lives, then giving becomes a natural byproduct of what we believe. Therefore, stewardship of who we are and all the resources we possess, which are given to us for safe keeping, is an act and extension of our worship. Leaders and laity alike are encouraged to heed the clarion call to become good stewards of all of God's resources.

---

[74] 2 Corinthians 9:7.

BISHOP L. W. III AND DR. NATALIE A. FRANCISCO

B ishop L. W. III and Dr. Natalie A. Francisco serve as Senior Pastors of Calvary Community Church and co-founders of Calvary Christian Academy in Hampton, VA. As President and Executive Vice President of Calvary Covenant Ministries, Inc., the culmination of their twenty-six years of experience in full-time ministry is shared from the perspective of providing spiritual oversight, leadership development, preaching, teaching, and administrative support to pastors and congregations across the United States as well as in Jamaica, West and South Africa, and the United Kingdom. In addition, they are the authors of several books: *The 21ˢᵗ Century Man* and *Get the Hell Out!* by L. W. Francisco III, D.Min.; and *Wisdom for Women of Worth and Worship, Parenting and Partnering with Purpose,* and *A Woman's Journal for Joyful Living* by Natalie A. Francisco, Ed.D.

Although Bishop and Dr. Francisco are actively involved in community service opportunities as directors on various local and national boards and have the privilege of mentoring many in ministry, their greatest joys are found in spending personal time with God and their beautiful daughters, Nicole, Lesley, and Lauren.

4

ON BECOMING A STEWARD LEADER

BY R. SCOTT RODIN

▨ INTRODUCTION—CAUTION FLAGS! ▨

The focus of this chapter is on the word "becoming." For that reason, we must raise some caution flags here at the beginning. We might be tempted to think that the process of becoming involves checklists and techniques that will result in a person becoming a steward leader. Far too many leadership books promise outcomes based on formulas and processes. Our human nature tends toward the recipe approach to success. We seek the ingredients and instructions needed to achieve our goals, believing that if it worked for others it should work for us.

If you like formulas, checklists, recipes, and methods, this chapter will likely frustrate you, or worse. In my journey of becoming a steward leader, I have been personally challenged at a deeper, more profound level than in any other undertaking in my life. The reason is that this journey encompasses the entirety of life. It is not an optional add-on to our other commitments as Christians. If we choose to walk this journey, it will fundamentally change the way we think, lead, and live.

The journey of becoming a steward leader is uncompromising, unequivocal, unrelenting, and unending. It is a journey of faith that God uses to transform hearts and equip men and women for faithful and effective service wherever they are called. This journey usually involves a movement in three parts: *discovery, commitment, and accountability.* Transformation begins with a *discovery* or new understanding about the nature of God and will of God for us. This is accompanied by the realization of how far we've fallen short, which leads us to the desire for change. That change is made effective in us by following disciplines to which we are *committed* in order for the change to take place in us. After discovery and commitment, there needs to be *accountability.* I cannot make this journey alone, nor am I supposed to. We are fellow travelers on the journey of faith, and we need each other to encourage and challenge us along the way. I will develop this chapter around these three parts of the journey of the steward leader.

■ I. DISCOVERY—ONE-KINGDOM LIVING ■

In order to become a steward leader, we must first discover what that term means and how it is distinct and unique from every other form of leadership we've been taught. I define a steward leader as *a one-kingdom steward who is called to lead.* We are first called to be one-kingdom stewards. From the moment that Christ became our Lord and Savior, we began a journey of transformation into one-kingdom stewards. The term *steward* marks our identity in Christ. Therefore, when we are called to lead, we can only do so as steward leaders. That is why the term *becoming* is so important. Just as our transformation into one-kingdom stewards is ongoing, so also is our journey to becoming steward leaders. They are, in fact, the same journey.

The theology of the one-kingdom steward is built on two amazing truths. **The first** is that you and I were created in the image of the God we know in Jesus Christ, who has revealed himself to us as the triune God of grace.

Scripture proclaims that we have been created in the image of a self-revealing, loving, triune God (Genesis 1:26–27; Colossians 1:15; Colossians 3:9–10). The implications are enormous, all-pervasive, and unequivocal. Here is the fruit of this amazing truth: when we know with certainty the nature of our Creator, God, and the image that we bear as his children, then we can know with equal certainty the purpose for our existence. This certainty leads us to a life that has meaning as we live out that purpose. It is an invitation to a new kind of life, to contentment, to real joy, and to freedom.

Questions for the Journey

- Do you believe that you know the heart and nature of your Creator with sufficiency and certainty in and through Jesus Christ? A steward must know the heart and will of the Master.
- If you know this certainty for yourself, then does your life reflect the image of a God who is, in his very nature, relationship, fellowship, and community? A steward must represent the heart of the master.

The second amazing truth is that God created us for rich and meaningful relationships on four levels: our relationships *with God, with ourselves, with our neighbors*, and *with creation*. At each level, Scripture reveals to us God's original intent, the devastating effects of sin, and the restoration accomplished in the work of Christ. Understanding this movement in salvation history is the key to discovering our call to be one-Kingdom stewards and steward leaders.

Stewarding the Gifts of God—The Three-fold Movement of Salvation History

If we look at the first three chapters of Genesis, we will discover the four levels of relationship that mark us as being created in God's image, as God's beloved creation. First, we were created for relationship *with God*. Loving God with our whole hearts is the primary purpose for our creation. Second, we were created for relationship *with our individual selves*. We were created to have an absolute certainty of who we are, why we are here, and what we are to do. Third, we were created for relationship *with our neighbors*. We are to love our neighbors as we love ourselves. That means seeing our neighbors' well-being in the same way we see our own. Fourth, we were created for relationship *with creation*. God put us in a beautiful garden and commanded us to take care of it and tend it. We were meant to live in harmony with creation—to love it, to tend it, to take care of it. As Adam and Eve lived out those four levels of relationship, they reflected the image of God (and so do we, when we do the same). This is the initial movement in salvation history, but the story does not end there.

When sin entered into the world, it had a devastating effect on our relationships at every level. Sin caused separation from God that could only be overcome through the blood of Christ. Sin also caused a loss of relationship with ourselves, our neighbors, and the creation that was designed for our nurture and enjoyment. Adam and Eve lost their sole purpose in life. In an instant, they went from walking with God in the evening and caretaking and tending his garden to dealing suddenly with God as a feared stranger who banished them from the only safe place they have ever known. The result was that Adam and Eve lost that sense of who they were—their sense of meaning. They had their primary purpose and vocation in life—fellowshipping with God and tending to his creation—thrown into disarray. The central theme of the history of humanity became our search to get back what was lost, to find God again and be at peace with ourselves, our neighbors, and creation.

But the story doesn't end there! The restoration that Christ came to accomplish through his own blood was even more holistic than the effects of the fall. All that was lost in the fall was *fully and completely* restored in Christ!

Our relationship with God was re-established. Through the blood of Christ, we have been reconciled to God. And that same reconciliation and restoration took place for us on the other three levels as well. Christ reclaimed for us a redeemed understanding of who we are as his children. We are now kingdom people, citizens of his kingdom, and children of the King. We have also been reconciled with our neighbors. The Great Commission and the Great Commandment call us to love one another and care for our neighbors. We've been called to the ministries of reconciliation, peacemaking, and servanthood. We are able to love our neighbors properly because we can now love ourselves as God's beloved—and redeemed—creation. And we have a redeemed relationship with creation. We see ourselves once again as both the crown of creation and one *with* creation. We are given back our true calling to care for and rule over the world with a loving and godly rule. This impacts our use of time, talents, and treasures, and it calls us into a true stewardship relationship with our environment.

The biblical truth about our nature and calling as stewards can be summed up in this way: *We were created to enjoy full relationships on four levels. Those relationships were destroyed through sin and restored through the work of Christ, and now they have been given back to us **as precious gifts for us to steward** with obedience and joy.*

The One-kingdom Steward

This brings us to the definition of our vocation as stewards: *We are stewards of our redeemed and restored relationships with God, with ourselves, with our neighbors, and with all of creation.*[75]

- We are stewards of our relationship with God, and we respond to this calling with obedience and joy by nurturing and deepening our relationship with God.
- We are stewards of our relationships with ourselves, and we respond to this calling with obedience and joy by seeking to always be in that God-pleasing balance of being precious and beloved by God and also humble, thankful, and obedient to his Word.
- We are stewards of our relationships with our neighbors, and we respond to this calling with obedience and joy by entering into caring, supportive, and loving relationships with one another, seeking to love our neighbors as ourselves, to work for peace and reconciliation.
- We are stewards of God's creation and all the material possessions that we have, and we respond to this calling with obedience and joy by caring for God's amazing creation and placing all of life in the service of the one Lord of the one kingdom.

The holistic image of the one-kingdom steward is our calling, and it can be described like this:

As God's people, we are called to reflect the image of our Creator, God, through whole, redeemed relationships with God, with ourselves, with our neighbors, and with all of creation, bringing glory to God and practicing in each relationship the ongoing work of the faithful steward.

Becoming a steward leader starts with this definition of a one-kingdom steward. As such, it is a theology of worship that is a joyful response to the God who is for us in Jesus Christ. A one-kingdom steward is a new creation in Christ. A one-kingdom steward is a joyous servant in the kingdom of God. A one-kingdom steward is a child of the

---

[75] See the chapter by Mark L. Vincent for more discussion on this subject.

King. A one-kingdom steward has a mission and a purpose in life. A one-kingdom steward is one who knows God in real, personal, certain terms and who knows that God is for us! And in all of this, a one-kingdom steward is free!

The Battle for Lordship

If our lives as God's stewards are lived out on all four levels, then we are living as one-kingdom stewards. A one-kingdom steward is someone who has submitted everything on all four levels to the full authority of the one Lord, who reigns over the one true kingdom: the kingdom of God.

The unfortunate reality is that none of us who claim Christ as our Lord are complete, committed, holistic, one-kingdom people. There are places in all of our lives where we hold back, grasp for control, and play the owner. We are tempted to begin to take little pieces of God's gifts to us and use them to build a second kingdom: *our* kingdom. We erect sturdy walls to protect all kinds of great stuff in our kingdoms. We may keep time, financial assets, relationships, our self-images, and more in our kingdoms.

We cannot be transformed into steward leaders until we acknowledge and confess that we are kingdom builders. It is only in this state of repentance and confession that we are ready to hear the voice of our Lord calling us to live for Christ—a call to give up *all* things in our earthly kingdoms. The great German theologian Dietrich Bonheoffer proclaimed it clearly, "When Christ calls a man, he bids him come and die."[76]

God is calling you to step off your throne and come into his kingdom fully, completely, and unequivocally. He is calling you to be a one-kingdom steward so that you can be equipped to be an effective steward leader.

He is calling you today, right now, at this very moment, to submit everything on all four levels to the full authority of the one Lord who reigns over the one kingdom of God. He is calling you to lay everything you have at the feet of one Lord in every area of your life. He is inviting you to step into your true calling as a one-kingdom steward.

---

[76] Dietrich Bonheoffer, *The Cost of Discipleship* (New York: The MacMillan Company, 1957), 73.

Once we have made this life-changing discovery, we are ready to consider our commitment in response.

■ II. COMMITMENT ■

Becoming a one-kingdom steward is a journey, not a destination. It starts with our acknowledgment that we are kingdom builders. It requires us to identify the stuff of our second kingdoms, searching the back hallways and locked closets where we hide away those secret things in our own kingdoms that we would just as soon not acknowledge. If they are left in hiding and not dragged out into the light, then when we are called into positions of leadership, they will become the raw material that the enemy will use to destroy us from within. If we will let him, the Holy Spirit will drive out all self-delusion when it comes to the stuff that remains in our own kingdoms. Becoming an effective steward leader means yielding ourselves to this cleansing process of becoming one-kingdom stewards.

At each of these four levels we have been given a gift, and we face a significant temptation. I will suggest here what that might look like at each one.

Level One—Intimacy with God

At the first level, we have been given the incredible gift of intimacy with God. The enemy counters with temptation of distraction. We fill our own kingdoms with the habits and practices of a frenetic lifestyle that so overwhelms us with things we must do that it robs us of true intimacy with God. There may be no greater battle that we will face as steward leaders than this. There are three tensions that are indicative of this battle.

Being vs. Doing

God is primarily concerned with *who we are,* not *what we do.* Throughout Scripture we learn that God seeks first the transformation of our hearts before the transaction of our business. There is a growing crisis in leadership among those who profess to be followers of Christ. It is not a lack of effort, passion, commitment, or training. Rather, the crisis lies deeper within the heart, and it can be summed up in this way: *We are so driven to "do" the work of God that we neglect the more important process of "being" the person God created us to be.*

Christian leaders are *doing* themselves to death! Believing that somehow God is pleased with a frenetic pace that leaves us exhausted, we take on more responsibility and shoulder more burdens for our people. We measure our success as leaders in quantitative terms, whether in business, social service, or ministry. However, the measurement of success in the kingdom of God is radically different. Jesus measures things like our thirst for intimacy with our heavenly Father, our love of ourselves as God created us, the quality of our relationships, and our care for his creation.

Matthew records in chapter 16:

> Then Jesus said to his disciples, "If anyone would come after me, he must deny himself and take up his cross and follow me. For whoever wants to save his life will lose it, but whoever loses his life for me will find it. What good will it be for a man if he gains the whole world, yet forfeits his soul? Or what can a man give in exchange for his soul?"

The denial of self for the sake of the cross calls us to lose our *doing-driven* life that measures our worth by the accumulation of our accomplishments. Jesus questions the value of a life of doing—*gaining the whole world*—if it costs us our very being—*losing your own soul.*

The apostle Paul writes, "If I speak in the tongues of men and of angels, but have not love, I am only a resounding gong or a clanging cymbal."[77] Paul points to the transformation of the heart as the normative and requisite transformation from which all of our acts of love must flow. Cut off from inner transformation, our outward acts, our very best *doing,* are reduced to *the resounding gong of a clanging cymbal.* It profits us nothing. It is empty and void of meaning.

The first calling of the steward leader is to "be" fully the person God created you to be. It is a life driven by a thirst to know deeper intimacy with God. It is the priority of *being* the godly leader over *doing* the work of leading.

Questions for the Journey

- Are you *doing-driven*?
- How do you measure your success?
- Do you value the work God seeks to do *within* you above all else?

---

[77] 1 Corinthians 13:1.

Producing vs. Bearing

As leaders, we are, by nature, producers. We are called upon to produce results, growth, disciples, profits, good employees, strategic plans, budgets, income, board reports, ideas, and more for our churches, our ministries, and our businesses. These are the fruits of our labors.

Consider, however, the kind of fruit the apostle John talks about in chapter 15 of his gospel:

> I am the true vine, and my Father is the gardener. He cuts off every branch in me that bears no fruit, while every branch that does bear fruit he prunes so that it will be even more fruitful. You are already clean because of the word I have spoken to you. Remain in me, as I also remain in you. No branch can bear fruit by itself; it must remain in the vine. Neither can you bear fruit unless you remain in me. I am the vine; you are the branches. If you remain in me and I in you, you will bear much fruit; apart from me you can do nothing.

Six times (and several more throughout the chapter) John refers to *bearing fruit.* I am convinced that the fruit John talks about is not the product of our labor but the outpouring of the Holy Spirit that only comes in our *abiding in the vine.* Instead of our fruitfulness measured in business terms, we are called to bear the fruit of the Spirit that is measured in kingdom terms. Paul described this fruit as "love, joy, peace, patience, kindness, goodness, faithfulness, gentleness, and self control."[78] The direction is clear; when we become completely surrendered and dependent on God, like a branch to a vine, the Holy Spirit can flow through us, producing in us this fruit. John pronounces this the "fruit that will last."

Our challenge as steward leaders is to ensure that our focus is on *bearing* the fruit of the Spirit rather than *producing* the fruit of our own hands. We are constantly expected to produce fruit in running our ministries, churches and businesses. However, our first and highest calling is not to *produce* but to *remain* or *abide.* It is only in daily abiding that God's Spirit can fill us, guide us, encourage us, discipline us, empower us, and equip us for our work. Once we try to do it on our own, we become "like a branch that is thrown away and withers; such branches are picked up, thrown into the fire and burned." These

---

[78] Galatians 5:22–23.

are strong words of warning for leaders who seek to work for God in their own strength.

Questions for the Journey

- What does it mean for you to *abide in the vine*?
- What is keeping you from focusing on *abiding* and *bearing* rather than *producing*?
- Is there evidence in your life that you are bearing the fruit of the Spirit?

Please don't take Jesus' admonition lightly. He said, "No branch can bear fruit by itself; it must remain in the vine. Neither can you bear fruit unless you remain in me ... apart from me you can do nothing." Nothing? Yes, *nothing* that is transformational, nothing that is filled with power and authority, nothing that changes lives, and nothing that endures.

The journey of the steward leader requires us to take to heart our call to bear the fruit of the Spirit first, before we put our hands to the work of producing the fruit of our ministries.

Steward vs. Owner

As stewards, we understand that all of life is on loan, and we respond by living lightly in this world as caretakers of that which is not ours. This results in a life of real freedom to which we respond with joyful obedience. These are the marks of the one-kingdom steward: freedom, obedience, and joy.

At battle with this freedom is an enemy who seeks to steal our joy by luring us into playing the owner. As owners, we claim to have control over our time, talents, and resources that we can employ for our own good and gain. Once we shift our perspective from steward to owner, we experience the loss of the carefree and become enslaved to the never-ending work of maintaining our control and gaining more of it.

This is the battle of our lives ... and it is a battle for lordship.

The stakes in this battle are greatly increased when we are called to lead. As leaders, we now fight this battle with and on behalf of others. And for the people we lead and the organizations we serve, everything depends on whether we choose to be owner leaders or steward leaders!

Owner leaders take their organization on their own shoulders and tie their own self-worth to its success, which requires that they protect turf, use people as a means to an end, and exert control over every situation. Their leadership is typified by power and fear and results in anxiety, stress, and burnout. They are leaders in bondage, and they, in turn, enslave the people they lead.

Steward leaders yield their organization to God and seek only to be an obedient, responsive servants of the true Owner. As a result, they are set free to lead! In this freedom they give away power and build up the people around them. They are at peace with success or struggle because they are at peace with themselves. And God works through them to set their people free.

As Christians who are called to lead, we are on a journey from our old ownership ways to the victorious life of the steward leader. The journey is marked by an almost continuous battle to let God to be the absolute Lord of our lives and of all aspects of our calling as leaders.

Questions for the Journey

- How are you faring in this battle? Where are you on this journey? The answers may be best found by asking your staff, your peers, your children, and your spouse.
- What would they say about your progress on this journey? Will you ask them?

Steward leaders who have found freedom in an intimate relationship with God can lead their people toward that same freedom. They will value and encourage the work God is doing in the hearts of their people and join them on a mutual journey of faith and discovery. And as they model the heart of a steward leader, they will cultivate a culture of generosity within the organizations they lead.

This world is desperately in need of steward leaders who have sold out completely to Jesus Christ, who stake no claims for themselves but rejoice in the success of everyone around them ... leaders who are genuinely free!

Disciplines for Intimacy

The process of becoming a steward leader will involve the discipline of seeking after and practicing those actions and habits that yield increasing levels of intimacy with God. This will likely require us to *stop doing* rather than start doing something new. The more we *do,* the more we fail to *be.*

- **Pray** that God would lead you to change your heart and your attitudes so that you will be equipped to value *being* over *doing.*
- **Ask God to develop** within you a passion for abiding in Him that will result in bearing the fruit of the Spirit.

The answers to these prayers are part of the journey you are on to becoming a one-kingdom steward who can be used by God to be a steward leader.

Level Two—Balance in my Identity

The second aspect of this gift is wholly dependent upon the first. Godly stewards have been given the gift of certainty in their knowledge of their own identity as the workmanship of this loving God, having been created in his image. This knowledge of our identity translates into the confidence that we were created to have a place and role in God's greater work. This is heady stuff! Our lives are not accidents.

Scripture sets up for us a tension in how we are to understand and steward this identity. *I believe that understanding and maintaining this tension is the single most challenging and important component in the life of the steward leader.*

Here is what this tension looks like: On one hand, we are assured that we are beloved children of God. We *are* "fearfully and wonderfully made."[79] We are truly "God's workmanship, created in Christ Jesus to do good works, which God prepared in advance for us to do."[80] Our lives have been bought with the blood of Christ so that we can be restored to intimacy and fellowship with the God who created us just to be with us.

The other side is just as real and certain. We are the redeemed yet still sinful children of God. For all of the grace and love showered down

---

[79] Psalm 139:14.
[80] Ephesians 2:10.

upon us, we have hearts that are still in need of the ongoing transformation of the Holy Spirit. We remain on the journey, and because we do, we still fall back into the old habits and sins of lives that are passing away, yet are still so very present. We live in an almost constant need of grace and forgiveness.

Our identity as one-kingdom stewards is found only in the very midst of this tension. Freedom is not the result of the easing of this tension, but when we can embrace both the wonder of our own creation and the depth of our own sin. We are free to look our sin in the face and not let it overwhelm us. And we are free to let God work wondrous and miraculous things in us and through us, without ever thinking that we alone are wonderful and miraculous. Becoming a steward leader is a process of finding this sweet spot, this place of maintained tension and enjoying the freedom that God has for us there.

It is in that sweet spot that steward leaders are free in relationship to their specific callings. They can wear their mantle of leadership lightly. Steward leaders must be free to truly be stewards of their people they serve and the organizations they lead. They must reject every temptation to play the owner and live and work daily in a freedom with respect to their current positions. This is not disengagement or aloofness but real freedom.

Confidence in your specific calling means confidence in God's ability to move you to a new place of challenge and fulfillment in his good time. We need to be committed to serving our organizations with our whole hearts and also be ready and free to leave them to our successors whenever God so leads, *all at the same time.*

The Temptation of Self-Confidence

The temptation we face in this journey of becoming a steward leader is the lure of *self*-confidence. The enemy wants us to be anything but confident in the heart of our creator, God. He wants us to be anywhere but in balance in our self-understanding and perception. And he wants us to do anything but lead with freedom. One way this self-confidence works its way in us is in our tendency to believe that our identity is really tied up in our success, the tangible product of our good leadership. Businesses assess the worth of their leaders according to the bottom line of profits and dividends. Political success is measured by re-election. Military leaders are measured by their disciplined execution of strategy. Even in ministry, our worth as leaders is too often measured by the size of our congregations, the growth of staff, or the expansion of our programs.

Our culture measures a person's worth in terms of productivity. Stated somewhat crassly, we are valued more for *what we do* than *who we are*. No wonder we are constantly tempted to veer off the path and focus on counterfeit sources of validation for our self-worth.

For leaders, the end result of listening to these voices is that we tie our self-worth—indeed, the validation for our existence—to the level of success we achieve as leaders. As such, our jobs take on cosmic significance, and our success as leaders becomes a matter of life and death. For this reason, we will sacrifice marriages and families and work ourselves into the grave for success. To preserve and protect our identities, we will use people, manipulate processes, grasp furiously at increasing our control, compromise our ethics, and ultimately, justify almost any behavior.

Then one day we wake up and realize that our self-worth is in the control of the uncontrollable. Our identity hangs by a thread over a chasm of discontent, and we are numbed by the realization that we have little say over what happens next. We have exchanged the truth of God for a lie. We have taken our eyes off the Author and Perfecter of our faith and lost sight of the only source of our true identity.

A friend of mine puts the question this way: "Who—as a matter of deep conviction and humility—will determine your worth, the value of your life on earth?"

Questions for the Journey

- Have you tied your identity to your job?
- Does your success in your job determine your sense of self-worth?
- Have you sacrificed things of great value in order to ensure your success?

A second way that self-confidence works to our ruin is in our need for affirmation. Every healthy, functioning person needs affirmation. As followers of Jesus, the affirmation that satisfies our spirits is the knowledge and certainty that our work is pleasing to God and our hearts are right toward Him. I have a bookmark that reads, "It doesn't matter if the world knows or sees or understands, the only applause we

BECOMING A STEWARD LEADER

are meant to seek is that of nail-scarred hands." God created us with spirits that can be fully satisfied by His never-ending, abundant, and loving affirmation of us. If we seek this, it will always fully satisfy us.

As leaders, we are tempted to search elsewhere for a counterfeit kind of approval. Our need for affirmation often increases in proportion to the demands of our jobs. The growing stress of work can drive us to seek increased affirmation. Slowly, but in a very real way, the desire for affirmation becomes an addiction; the more applause we get, the more we hunger for it.

In our drive to feed this addiction, what almost always suffers is our intimacy with God. We become so busy *doing* the work God called us to do that we stop spending time *with* God. In order to keep feeding our addiction to approval, we stop feeding our souls.

When our intimate life with God suffers, our need for affirmation will never be satisfied. And when the level of affirmation from our jobs no longer meets our needs, when possessions, power, and popularity no longer satisfy, we will turn to more illicit fascinations that offer the satisfaction we seek. Sexual sin, greed, and other moral failings are the collateral damage caused by a storm system fueled by the desperate search for a counterfeit form of affirmation. When intimacy with God is lost, the enemy will supply all the ingredients necessary for our destruction.

Questions for the Journey

- Where do you receive the affirmation you need in your life?
- Is the certain knowledge that Jesus loves you and that you are a beloved child of God enough for you? If not, why not?
- Where have you listened to counterfeit voices of affirmation, and what are they doing to your spirit?

Steward leaders who maintain balance in their identity before Christ will develop whole people who are balanced and healthy in their own self-perceptions. They will harness the true power of their people, enabling and encouraging the greatest level of achievement and excellence from their people and building the most faithful and effective organizations as a result.

Disciplines for Balance

I would suggest three disciplines to help you maintain the balance of the effective steward leader. The first is *examining your self* to identify the warning signs in your own life as a leader. As leaders, we must gather around us people who will tell us the truth about ourselves. Have them help you look for signs of an ownership attitude and challenge the ways they see you tying your self-image to success. Surround yourself with people who will be honest with you to keep you humble in the face of success, ensuring you seek only one source for the applause you desire to hear. Look deeply into the mirror, unstop your ears, listen to the voices of friends and foes alike, and do not fall prey to the deception that all of this is somehow below you.

The second discipline is the *cry for help*. We cannot heal ourselves. To whatever level there is imbalance in your life and work, that is the level to which you need help to recover the place of calm that your spirit so desperately seeks. It only takes a simple admission and request. You can say, "Lord, I am losing the battle and playing the owner, and it is overwhelming me. I can't get out. Can you help me? Lord, I've listened to the voices of others to fulfill my need for affirmation for so long I don't know how to stop. Can you help me get out? Lord, my whole self-esteem is tied to my success, and it is weighing me down and about to crush me. Can you set me free?" These are the prayers of the leaders for whom balance is about to be restored.

The third discipline may be the hardest. It requires us to *believe*. When we have named the ingredients that plague our souls and when we have made the cry for help that moves us beyond ourselves and refocuses our attention on God, we then must simply believe. *Expect* God to act. Expect that He hears our cries and will not leave us helpless. *Remember* that He loves us, that He is for us, that He gave His life for us, and that His promises are unequivocal.

God works miracles in the heart that believes. With belief comes trust and submission to His will. Let Him begin to work in you: in your attitudes, your false pride, your selfishness, your blind spots, and your fears. Trust Him to walk with you on this journey, for that's what it is. The course that leads us out of the storm is a journey of deepening faith, greater trust, genuine humility, and abundant grace.

- **Pray** that God will empower you to keep your eyes focused on him and your ears open to hear his words of affirmation so that no other voice but his will be heard.
- **Ask God to develop** in you a deep sense of certainty and security in resting your identity, your reputation, and your success in Him and Him alone.

Level Three—Presence with my Neighbor

At this third level we can now recognize how integrated is this journey of becoming a steward leader. Intimacy with God gives us the certainty of who we are and why we are here. Our vocations and identities flow from this relationship with our Creator. What follows is that we can only love ourselves if we have that intimacy with God. As we do, we are able to live freely and therefore live in relationship with and truly love our neighbors.

Loving our neighbors as we love ourselves only happens as a result of the first two parts of our journey. The temptations we faced at those two levels prove devastating when we begin to consider how we interact with our neighbors. If all I care about is producing, then my neighbors (peers, co-workers, friends, etc.) become a means of production. My relationships become centered on answering the question, "How can you help me achieve what I need to succeed in life?" Our relationships become utilitarian. People become means to an end. How else could fruit *producers* see relationships?

It's only when we submit ourselves fully to be branches, when we really realize that God calls us not to *produce* fruit but to *bear* fruit so that the Holy Spirit may flow through us and change the way we see and value our relationships. When we bear fruit, we have a chance to touch the lives of the people around us because they become ends in themselves. We cannot love our neighbors and be fruit producers in this world.

The same is true if we are owner leaders. If I believe that I own my organization, if I have to control what has to happen in my organization in order for things to happen, then I am going to need to control others. I cannot love you as my neighbor and seek to control you at the same time. If I need to manipulate you in order to get out of you what I need so that my organization can be successful, I can't also love you the way Christ wants me to love you. If we're owner leaders, we can't love our neighbors. The owner leader who is driven to produce will wreak havoc on his or her organization. Leaders who are bent on producing, getting bottom-line results, who own their organizations, who tie their reputations to the success of the organizations that they lead, will tear their organizations apart.

Questions for the Journey

- To what degree am I driven to produce?
- To what degree do I own my organization?
- What does it mean to love my neighbor as part of my journey to becoming a steward leader?

Loving our neighbors starts by realizing that every single person is on his or her own unique journey with God. God is calling and wooing and working in the lives of everyone we come in contact with every day. None of us live in a static moment. We're all becoming transformed daily into the image of Christ.

Questions for the Journey

- Do we see the people in our lives in static moments, or do we deal with them as co-travelers on a journey of faith?
- If I were to talk to your friends, your brothers and sisters, your co-workers, your parents, your spouses, your children, what kind of relationships would you want to be known for?
- How should we live among and with our neighbors if we believe that we're all in this process of transformation and we're called to help one another, to bless one another on that journey?

Steward leaders will build strong communities because they value them as ends in themselves and measure their worth to the organizations in kingdom terms. Their organizations will be effective because they see their leadership role as that of caretakers that cultivate organizational health, culture, and vision.

Disciplines for Presence

Becoming a steward leader at this third level is all about vision. It's about changing the way in which we look at one another.

- **Pray** each day for eyes to see your neighbors as God sees them.
- **Ask God to develop** within you the heart of a fellow traveler and for the freedom to be used by God to bless others on that journey. It requires new eyesight. It requires that we be free as steward leaders. It means entering with love into the journey of the people who are around us so we may be co-journeyers, co-travelers, so that we might bring blessing into the lives of the people around us. That kind of equipping can only come from the Holy Spirit working in us.

Level Four—Consistency in my Care of Creation

Everything we possess in this world has come from a simple combination of the human being created in God's image and the garden, which was created for the human—and the human for it. Those ingredients are the foundation for everything that exists in all of God's creation: a man, a woman, and a garden. Sometimes we make things too complicated. God said to Adam and Eve, "You love me, and I love you. Cherish each other. Tend the garden."

God has not changed, nor have his simple commands. After the redemption of all things in Christ, God still says to us, "I love you, and you love me. Love one another. Care for my creation." The key here, again, for the steward leader is freedom. When you can truly be free in your relationships from the lure of materialism and wealth and the power and prestige they bring, you can then lead others to freedom and joy. When you can stand in a peaceful relationship to time, neither serving it like a taskmaster nor wasting it like a sluggard but enjoying it and investing yourself in it freely, you can free your people to accomplish incredible things for the kingdom. When you can stand in a free relationship to money as its steward, when God is the sole lord of your possessions and they hold no sway over you, you can set your people free!

On this fourth level, like none of the others, steward leaders are in the battle of their lives. This is the enemy's territory. The steward leader stands as a warrior in the battle for the hearts and allegiance of God's people, starting with his and her own. Nowhere will the steward leader experience the frontal attack of the enemy more than here.

Becoming a steward leader means we will plan for it, prepare for it, and pray over it. We will be prepared for this battle personally so that we will be able to lead our people to victory in their own battles. The steward leader advancing on this fourth level will likely be shot at from both sides. We will battle with the enemy from without as we strive to live freely in a world where money, possessions, and power are all that matter. And we will battle an enemy from within, when those from our own ranks will question our commitment because we choose to love and care for the creation that God loves, which was our original mandate, vocation, calling, and joy.[81]

The gift given to the steward leader to fight this good and worthy fight is the gift of nurture. This gift of nurture is holistic, involving the entirety of God's good creation. This includes the stewarding of God's gift of time, God's investment in us of skills and talents that align with his calling, and God's provision for us through resources to meet our needs. This nurture requires that we are constantly being transformed as godly stewards, able to carry out the charge to have dominion over, rule over, and subdue as the very hands and feet of Christ.

The temptation is to forsake our role as nurturing stewards and to retake control. More than at any other level, this fourth level is where our kingdom building tendencies tempt us the most. Simply put, nurture is *others-centered,* and control is wholly *self-serving.* This is a struggle for lordship! We want control because we can use it to serve our selves. We grow up believing that there is nothing scarier than being *out of control.* As we grow wiser, we learn that there may be nothing more terrifying than the consuming desire to be in control of everything!

The call to nurture involves time, talents, and possessions, and we will face the temptation to control each area of our lives and work. In my twenty-seven years in working in ministry, I haven't encountered any force more damnable than the desire to gain control of every sphere of life. Steward leaders reject the belief that with control comes security, power, and peace. They know it is a clever and heinous deception. In their freedom they choose to nurture their relationships as stewards on this fourth level, and they help free their people to do the same. As a result, steward leaders marshal resources effectively, including the time, talents, potential, and assets of their people and their organizations. They strive for a coherent commitment to faithful stewardship throughout their organization, from strategic planning, to fundraising,

---

[81] Mark L. Vincent provides further description of the hideous enemies of the steward in his chapter.

to budgeting, to setting policy and casting vision for the future. When the world looks at their organizations, they see a consistent witness to godly stewardship on all four levels.

Disciplines for Consistency

Richard Kriegbaum writes the following in his leadership prayer concerning ownership,

> This is my one incessant prayer to you, hour by hour, day upon day: It's yours. I am not fighting this battle for you, God. It's your battle, and you are fighting it for me. It is all yours and I want whatever you have for me in this situation. It is not my organization, it is yours. So I depend on your Spirit to show me what to do. These are not my people. I chose them and organized their efforts, but they do not belong to me … So this day is yours; I am yours; these people are yours; the resources are yours. The challenges we face are yours, as is anything we hope to accomplish. It's yours, God. It is not mine.[82]

- **Pray** this prayer every morning. It is a prayer of freedom. It is the level of complete submission that we must all yearn for if we are to be steward leaders for our people and our organizations at this fourth level.
- **Ask God to develop within you** a watchful spirit that will alert you to the signs that your attitudes are slipping into an ownership/control mindset. You will know it by its companions: fear, anxiety, compulsion, envy, mistrust, selfishness, and impatience. These are signs that we have stopped submitting and started grasping, controlling, and seeking to play the owner. They are bondage.

▄ III. ACCOUNTABILITY ▄

I will close with a few words about accountability. We have said all the way along that we do not journey alone. If there is a final place where the enemy can find space to infiltrate a strong and sure defense, it is in the quiet contentment that comes from the self-delusion that we need no one's help on this journey. There has been much written about the importance of accountability, and it is one of those things toward

---

[82] Richard Kriegbaum, *Leadership Prayers* (Tyndale, 1998), 6–7.

which we all politely smile and nod our heads in agreement. Yet few of us have developed true accountability processes that have the authority and permission to challenge at the levels required of a truly effective steward leader.

Perhaps the reason we do not have such processes in place is because in our heart of hearts we do not like asking for help. We see asking as a sign of weakness and vulnerability. Our egos get in the way. Yet isolation is one of the great enemies of effective leadership. Talk to any leader who has suffered through a moral failing and you will hear a tale of withdrawal and isolation. Without accountability, we are free to deceive ourselves, trust in flawed perspectives, avoid tough questions, and remain unchecked and unchanged. In short, without account-ability, we stop traveling on the journey of becoming more effective steward leaders. We sit at the side of the road and become spectators, or worse, we become obstacles in the way of others on the same journey.

When it comes to asking for help, I have had no more profound experience then when I recently participated in a challenge course with my business colleagues and one exercise had us blindfolded and placed in a maze constructed of ropes. We were told to hold on with both hands and work our way through the maze to find the way out.

The young lady who administered this particular challenge walked around us saying, "Raise your hand if you have a question or need help getting out of the maze." At first, this seemed like a polite but unneces-sary offer. For fifteen minutes, I groped my way around in a futile attempt to find the way out. Finally, it became apparent that there was no physical way out of the maze. The entire perimeter was closed. Suddenly, her offer became more important. After asking several rather pathetic self-help questions, the solution dawned on me. This wasn't a physical challenge but a test to see if we would continue to rely solely on ourselves to our absolute infuriation. I humbly raised my hand, and when she came over, I said, "Megan, I can't get out of the maze. Can you help me?"

At once, she lifted the mask from my eyes, smiled, and said quietly, "Congratulations, you're out."

As leaders, we can become so confident in our own abilities that we will stumble around in the dark for years, even decades, before reaching the point where we are exhausted, lost, and failing. That does not need to be so. Becoming a steward leader is all about freedom. That begins with the freedom to be wrong, to be questioned, to be held accountable, to be vulnerable, and to fail. It is only our ownership attitudes that will keep us from developing accountability systems.

Accountability applies to our commitment to practice the disciplines outlined in this chapter. Here is my own word of accountability for you: The daily disciplines must begin before we leave our beds. It is the awakening prayer that follows our praise to God, our thanks for the day, and our placing our loved ones into the care of our loving God. The prayer we must pray is this one:

> I acknowledge today that life, identity, job, relationships, successes, possessions, the creation itself, that none of it is mine Lord; it is all yours. Grant me the heart of a one-kingdom steward, the courage and humility of a steward leader, and freedom and joy as a child of the King.

Don't leave your bed without it! Once we start the routines of our days, our ownership and control tendencies come rushing in. We need to enter each day in our freedom, prepared to live in joyful obedience. To break the cycle of ownership and control, we must not leave our beds until our hearts are free. It is easier to reject a temptation in our freedom than to unburden ourselves of it once it has already climbed aboard.

You may need to keep this prayer close at hand and pray it often throughout each day. Memorize it, and discipline yourself to recognize bondage attitudes and attack them at the onset with the freedom of absolute submission. Then claim for yourself the promise, *"It is for freedom that Christ has set us free"* (Galatians 5:1 emphasis mine).

Welcome to the journey!

Scott Rodin

S cott Rodin has been serving not-for-profits organizations for the past twenty-eight years, providing counsel in fundraising, leadership development, and strategic planning to over one hundred organizations in the US, Canada, the Middle East, Great Britain, and Australia. He is a Partner and Head of Strategic Alliances with Artios Partners, a training and resourcing organization equipping leaders for excellence in stewarding Christian organizations, churches, and ministries. He is also a Senior Fellow of the Engstrom Institute.

Dr. Rodin is past president of the Christian Stewardship Association and was formerly the president of Eastern Baptist Theological Seminary in Philadelphia. He serves on the Boards of China Source and the Evangelical Environmental Network.

Dr. Rodin holds Master of Theology and Doctor of Philosophy degrees in Systematic Theology from the University of Aberdeen, Scotland. His books include *The Third Conversion, The Steward Leader, The Sower, The Four Gifts of the King, The Seven Deadly Sins of Christian Fundraising,* and *Abundant Life and Stewards in the Kingdom.*

Dr. Rodin is married to Linda, and they reside in Spokane, Washington.

5

STEWARD LEADERS ARE SOWERS: TEN INSIGHTS FOR ENCOURAGING CHRISTIAN GENEROSITY

GARY G. HOAG

Steward leaders of non-profit organizations and churches have a tough job. They are spiritually gifted to lead, and they do that tirelessly. Simultaneously, they are expected by their governing boards to ensure the ministry has adequate resources to meet current and future needs. In a word, they are expected to *provide*.

Because the job requires the bandwidth of more than one person, steward leaders appoint staff to help. Some deliver programs: doing work such as sharing the gospel of Jesus Christ, feeding the hungry, teaching students, or caring for the sick. Others help rally support, such as intercessory prayer, volunteer service, and financial partnership.

When I started my professional career, I realized that though I could do the program work, my gifts best fit in rallying support. I believed it was my job to provide for the needs of the ministry. To that end, I employed whatever strategies I could find for raising money from people to provide for the work of the ministry. At times, I found the work rewarding and other times, downright dreadful.

In reflecting on this tension, my *a-ha* moment was coming to the realization that it was God's job, not mine, to provide for the needs of the ministry. In texts such as the Sermon on the Mount, I learned that Jesus instructed His disciples not to worry about even their most basic needs—food, drink, and clothing—but taught them to depend on God the Father to provide.[83] I also came to understand that God could be trusted to provide for the needs of the ministry I served because it belonged to him anyway. So what was my job in all this?

I came to see that my role as a steward leader was to be a sower: to sow truth in peoples' lives,[84] to show people ways they could participate with God by using the gifts He had given them to serve, by committing some time for prayer, and by sharing the funds He had entrusted to them as stewards. My job shifted from asking people for money and trying to *close* gifts to telling spiritual truths to stewards, which *opened* them to growing as givers.

This realization fueled my passion to sow in the hearts of stewards the amazing truth that they have the privilege of participating with God in His work. Simultaneously, I got to pray daily and trust God to provide for my needs and the needs of the ministry.

The steward leader in the New Testament who has helped develop my understanding of this is the apostle Paul. He did not try to make the gospel known throughout the ancient world on his own, utilizing the ancient system of raising money. He attended to God's work and rallied stewards to join him. If you count them, Paul had about forty people serving with him, doing work such as preaching and teaching, and about forty partners whose support and aid helped fuel ministry in the ancient world.[85]

Why highlight Paul as a role model? Here are two reasons. First, he was a steward leader with a job similar to the complex roles many ministry leaders have today. He had the privilege of sowing truth in the hearts of many fellow servants and supporters. Second, in his correspondence with the Corinthian Church related to taking up a collection for the Jerusalem Church, he shared the theology that guided his practice. That theology can aid us as well.

---

[83] Matthew 6:25–34.

[84] See the book I co-authored with R. Scott Rodin, *The Sower: Redefining the Ministry of Raising Kingdom Resources* (Winchester, VA: ECFA Press, 2010). Two other books largely influenced my thinking: Wesley K. Willmer, *God & Your Stuff: The Vital Link Between Your Possessions and Your Soul* (Colorado Springs: NavPress, 2002); Henri J.M. Nouwen, *The Spirituality of Fundraising* (New York: Henri Nouwen Society, 2004).

[85] Many of these names can be found in Romans 16 and Colossians 4:7–17, among other NT passages.

From my study of Paul's Corinthian correspondence, ten insights emerge for Steward Leaders who desire to encourage Christian generosity. They are for everyone who wishes to sow this profound truth: *stewards were made to participate with God in His work with the gifts, goods, and grace they have received from Him.*

■ TEN INSIGHTS FOR SOWERS FROM 1 CORINTHIANS 16:1–4 AND 2 CORINTHIANS 8–9 ■

Paul ministered in Corinth, and many became Christians there. To encourage and instruct them in the faith, he wrote two letters that have survived to this day and become part of the New Testament: 1 and 2 Corinthians. To mine passages in these ancient letters for insights for modern application is to seek to uncover principles that can be applied in as many different settings as steward leaders find themselves. Before reading the rest of this chapter, I invite you to read these two texts, 1 Corinthians 16:1–4 and 2 Corinthians 8–9, from which I have located ten insights for steward leaders today.

■ 1. STEWARD LEADERS DIRECT CHRISTIANS TO GIVE WHEN NEEDS ARISE. ■

> Now about the collection for the Lord's people: Do what I told the Galatian Churches to do. On the first day of every week, each one of you should set aside a sum of money in keeping with your income, saving it up, so that when I come no collections will have to be made.
>
> —1 Corinthians 16:1–2

Most people think that Paul *asked* the Corinthians to give to help those in need in Jerusalem. Interestingly, Paul did not *ask* them, he *directed* them to send aid. In *The Message*, Eugene Peterson succinctly states: "You get the same instructions I gave the Churches in Galatia." This directive came in the form of written instructions that clearly and concisely told the Christians in Corinth to set aside money for struggling saints in Jerusalem.

A closer look at these verses reveals Paul's role in calling for this collection. Paul simply communicates the need and instructs people to give. W. Graham Scroggie asserts, "There is nothing here of the frantic and sensational appeals which are today so frequent."[86] He did not use guilt to motivate them. Paul neither plays his apostolic authority trump card to force them to give, nor does he sheepishly ask them to give. To give or not to give is *not* the question here. He *directs* them to give, and the basis for his authority in extending these instructions is God's blessing in their lives. As they prospered, in keeping with their income, they were to share with needy Christians.

Shortly thereafter, Clement of Rome (c. 96 C.E.) echoed Paul's perspective, providing similar instruction in his letter to the Corinthians regarding aiding needy Christians in Rome: "Let the one who is strong take care of the weak; and let the weak show due respect to the strong. Let the wealthy provide what is needed for the poor, and let the poor offer thanks to God, since he has given him someone to supply his need."[87]

In Paul's communication regarding the collection, he models two activities for future steward leaders, from Clement of Rome to us today. First, he demonstrates that strategic planning is an important facet of the work. Orchestrating this collection effort required advance communication, a coordinated response in Corinth, and a concerted effort that would link together many churches in other cities to participate.

Second, he showed that the responsibility of the steward leader is to sow truth in the lives of those you serve. Specifically, he taught what God's people do in tough times. He did not force them to obey, beg from them, or try to control their responses. He merely gave instructions on aiding fellow believers in trouble.

At this point, it is important to note that in hierarchical societies, such as the East, when leaders give instructions, often indirectly or through a culture broker, followers tend to follow the will of the leadership. In more individualistic societies, like the West, it is different. Leaders tend to be more direct, and those they serve are more self-centered. Because hearers do not necessarily follow the instructions of their leaders as readily, Western leaders often employ strategies that go beyond communication to manipulation in order to get the responses

---

[86] W. Graham Scroggie, *The Unfolding Drama of Redemption* (Grand Rapids: Kregel, 1994), 100.

[87] 1 Clement 38.2. Clement, Bishop of Rome urged the Christians in Corinth to live out their faith in words *and* deeds. Christians with more than enough were to share with those who did not have enough.

they seek. Additionally, those in the South tend to be more group-oriented and more sensitive to the needs of others, which means they may not follow instructions until everyone is on board as a group.

Why sketch these cultural distinctions? The way in which instructions or directives are given varies in different cultural settings. The point to apply globally is this: *when needs surface in the community of faith, steward leaders instruct God's people to share as they are able to help those in need.* They sow this truth in a manner that is culturally appropriate. In doing so, they connect those who need help with those who can help.

■ 2. STEWARD LEADERS PERSONALLY SEE TO IT THAT GIVING IS ADMINISTERED WITH INTEGRITY. ■

> Then, when I arrive, I will give letters of introduction to the men you approve and send them with your gift to Jerusalem. If it seems advisable for me to go also, they will accompany me.
>
> —1 Corinthians 16:3–4

Before the days of online credit card gifts, electronic funds transfers from bank accounts, or even checks in the mail, cash contributions had to be collected and carried by hand. To do this, leaders appointed trusted people, used carefully outlined processes, and demonstrated a willingness to serve to get the job done.

According to Paul, approved leaders would be needed to deliver the collection. They undoubtedly had a reputation of faithfulness to perform tasks in the church in Corinth, which qualified them for the job. In modern settings, it is critical to have faithful people processing charitable giving. Whether your ministry relies on thousands or millions of dollars in support each year, you must appoint trusted people to administer charitable giving. Don't stop there, though.

Steward leaders also implement processes for ensuring proper gift administration, because as John Stott put it, "The handling of money is risky business."[88] In the example of the Corinthian collection, the process for ensuring the faithful handling of the gift was to have more than one person involved. A team effort would ensure that no one person would be put in a place where he or she would be tempted to

---

[88] John R.W. Stott, *Stott on Stewardship: Ten Principles on Christian Giving* (Chattanooga, TN: Generous Giving, 2003), 9.

steal or misappropriate this gift. For it to make it to Jerusalem, a team would carry the load. Likewise, steward leaders today should implement processes and us people with appropriate controls to be sure gifts are handled with integrity.

Lastly, Paul models the posture of service for steward leaders. He expresses a willingness to help deliver this gift, if necessary. He wants the Corinthians to have the opportunity to participate through giving and will personally do whatever it takes to facilitate this act of worship.

In the ancient world, leaders would promise people honor and glory to receive gifts from them, but Paul does not go there. He does not offer perks for their participation. In so doing, he sets aside the rules of benefaction that governed giving in antiquity and, instead, subverts the system. He did what secular leaders in his day would not think of doing. He humbly offers up himself in sacred service, not seeking anything in return.

As a steward leader, you would be wise to take the posture of the humble servant in administrating charitable giving. Do this regardless of what the culture around you dictates. Mother Teresa grasped this, as captured in her own words: "If sometimes our poor people have had to die of starvation, it is not because God didn't care for them, but because you and I didn't give, were not instruments of love in the hands of God, to give them that bread, to give them that clothing; because we did not recognize him, when once more Christ came in distressing disguise—in the hungry man, in the lonely man, in the homeless child, and seeking for shelter."[89] What a remarkable, humble servant! She, who rallied millions to awareness and care for the poor, led by example.

■ 3. SACRIFICIAL GIVING IS THE RESULT OF GOD'S WORK, NOT THE STEWARD LEADER'S WORK. ■

> And now, brothers and sisters, we want you to know about the grace that God has given the Macedonian Churches. In the midst of a very severe trial, their overflowing joy and their extreme poverty welled up in rich generosity. For I testify that they gave as much as they were able, and even beyond their ability. Entirely on their own, they urgently pleaded with us for the privilege of sharing in this service

---

[89] Mother Teresa of Calcutta, *Gift for God: Prayers and Meditations* (San Francisco: HarperCollins, 1996), 24.

to the Lord's people. And they exceeded our expectations: They gave themselves first of all to the Lord, and then by the will of God also to us. So we urged Titus, just as he had earlier made a beginning, to bring also to completion this act of grace on your part. But since you excel in everything—in faith, in speech, in knowledge, in complete earnestness and in the love we have kindled in you—see that you also excel in this grace of giving.

—2 Corinthians 8:1–7

In this excerpt from Paul's second letter to the Corinthians, it is clear that the Corinthian Church had not completed the task of taking up a collection for the church in Jerusalem. Interestingly, Paul does not remind them of how much is still needed. Why? I think because it was not about the money. On the contrary, he tells a story about sacrificial givers and describes sacrificial giving, not from a financial perspective but from a spiritual angle.

The story is about the Macedonians. While little is known about their suffering, we know this about them: They gave joyfully of their own free will at a level that was unpredictably generous. Why? It was not tied to how Paul wrote his appeal letter. Their deep desire to give sacrificially and share in this service to those in need flowed out of God's work in their lives, not Paul's.

Steward leaders often read this passage as encouraging friendly competition or as condoning arm-twisting tactics to motivate giving. A closer look at the culture does reveal that competition between cities would help them gain prominence in the ancient world. However, if that was Paul's motive, he probably would have etched an inscription in Corinth, noting the amount of their giving, for the purpose of coercing them to participate.

Paul does not try to manipulate them in sharing about the Macedonians because it is not about competition. He uses them as an example to teach the Corinthians about giving. Paul celebrates the only kind of giving Jesus celebrated: sacrificial giving (cf. Mark 12:41–44). He then moves the conversation from the financial to the spiritual.

At this point, ministry leaders often say, "Then how do you ask people to give?" Since giving shifts from a financial conversation to a spiritual one, my general rule is to move from: "Will you make a gift to this ministry project?" to "Will you ask God what sacrificial giving looks like for you?" The former question seeks to *close* people, to get them to give to you. The latter question *opens* people to give to God and follow His leading for the handling of the resources in their stewardship.

Think of it this way: As a steward leader, you cannot ask people to give what they do not own, you can only challenge them to be stewards who are faithful to follow the Master's instructions. In taking this position for those you serve, you will follow Paul's example and help them to grow in the grace of giving.

■ 4. SOMETIMES STEWARD LEADERS FOLLOW UP WITH PEOPLE AND REMIND THEM TO GIVE. ■

> And here is my judgment about what is best for you in this matter. Last year you were the first not only to give but also to have the desire to do so. Now finish the work, so that your eager willingness to do it may be matched by your completion of it, according to your means.
> —2 Corinthians 8:10–11

People often need to be reminded to fulfill giving commitments. This was true in the ancient world and is evident today. Though the text does not explain why they had not completed the collection, Paul's advice in his second letter is simply to get it done.

Reminding people is hard work, because you are repeating your efforts. Leaders often ask themselves: *Why did they not respond to my instructions the first time? Did they miss the message? Do I need to use bold letters, underlining, and a P.S. next time?* These questions point leaders down the path of mistakenly thinking that generosity flows as a result of their work rather than God's work and that encouraging generosity is about employing tactics that control outcomes, when it should be about addressing heart attitudes. Changes at the heart level take time; that's why grace must be extended to all.

Often the lack of participation in giving or failure to complete financial commitments is because people have not planned for it. Dan Busby believes, "Giving doesn't just happen. Most of us don't give as much as we should because we don't plan our giving. You may need to make some tough financial decisions in order to have the freedom to give more. You may need to reduce your debt load or opt for a simpler lifestyle. You might need a budget. It will certainly mean having a priority list, planning and keeping records. Remember, you are handling God's money."[90]

Most would agree that many in the modern world have not been taught how to be faithful managers of God's money. Teaching and modeling stewardship principles is part of the role of the steward leader, and again, this takes time. According to the research of Bruce Longenecker on the collection for the church in Jerusalem, it took over five years.[91, 92] This work requires grace and patience.

Paul demonstrates grace and patience in offering his judgment rather than exercising his authority. He wants their response to come from a willing heart. He is showing he cares more about their spiritual growth than the money. He knows that if generosity happens, it will flow from God's work in their lives; thus, his gracious tone toward the Corinthians echoes his words to the Galatians; Paul said to "remember the poor."[93]

▪ 5. ACCEPTABLE GIVING IS TIED TO WHAT STEWARDS HAVE, NOT WHAT THEY DON'T HAVE. ▪

> For if the willingness is there, the gift is acceptable according to what one has, not according to what one does not have.
>
> —2 Corinthians 8:12

Notice that Paul does not make a specific solicitation. Instead, he provides clear instructions on acceptable giving. Steward leaders would be wise to follow his example. Paul invites the Corinthians to take the inward journey of taking inventory of all God has given them and then to embark on an outward journey of freely blessing others from what they have.

Why is this so important? It may have been the cause for their delay in completing the collection. We don't know for sure. What we do know is that Paul addresses a common question givers ask themselves: "How much should I give?"

---

[90] Dan Busby, *Giving from the Heart: A Legacy that Lasts Forever* (Winchester, VA: Evangelical Council for Financial Accountability, 2008), 3.

[91] c. 53–58 C.E.

[92] Bruce W. Longenecker, *Remember the Poor: Paul, Poverty and the Greco-Roman World* (Grand Rapids: Eerdmans, 2010), 338–344.

[93] cf. Galatians 2:10.

C.S. Lewis said, "I do not believe one can settle on how much we ought to give. I am afraid the only safe rule is to give more than we can spare."[94] In a word, Lewis would say Christians should give *sacrificially.*

Ultimately, Paul wants the Corinthians to be found faithful in using God's resources in their stewardship. He shows steward leaders the kinds of conversations to have with givers, pointing them toward think about giving from what they have.

To move beyond superficial talk to topics like this, you must be committed to such a course for your own life. If you find this difficult teaching, take a few minutes before reading on, and take inventory of yourself. How are you using the gifts and goods in your stewardship? I have found this exercise leads to my own ongoing transformation and actually positions me to help others on the journey.

■ 6. STEWARD LEADERS DESCRIBE CHRISTIAN GIVING AS SHARING THAT LEADS TO EQUALITY. ■

> Our desire is not that others might be relieved while you are hard pressed, but that there might be equality. At the present time your plenty will supply what they need, so that in turn their plenty will supply what you need. The goal is equality, as it is written: "The one who gathered much did not have too much, and the one who gathered little did not have too little."
>
> —2 Corinthians 8:13–15

Paul cites the manna account from Exodus to share the purpose for the redistribution of resources: so that everyone has enough. When God's people were somewhere between the bondage of Egypt and the freedom of the Promised Land, they needed food to eat. God provided manna six days a week, and double what they needed the day before the Sabbath so that they could rest that day but still have enough to eat. He was their faithful Provider, but His provision came with a test.

They were not to store up more than they needed each day. If they did, it would spoil. In doing so, they would also demonstrate, vertically speaking, a lack of trust in God to provide the next day and, horizontally speaking, a lack of concern for their neighbor, who invariably might not get enough because of their hoarding.

---

[94] Lesley Walmsley, ed., "Social Morality" in *C.S. Lewis Essay Collection and Other Short Pieces* (London: HarperCollins, 2000).

BECOMING A STEWARD LEADER

The goal of gathering and redistributing manna was to be sure everyone had enough. Those who gathered much got to share with those who gathered little so everyone had enough. In Paul's thinking, Christian giving happens when those with more than enough share with Christians who have less than enough, because the goal is equality. The goal is for everyone to have enough.

Paul is graciously teaching the Corinthians *and us* to have concern for others. To teach this, we must first live it. Personally, I have found that I have been guilty of sinning both vertically and horizontally. For much of my life, I hoarded more than enough money and possessions rather than sharing them with Christians with less than enough. This showed both a disregard for God's teachings and a lack of concern for brothers and sisters in Christ in need around the world. In obedience to God, my wife and I decided to quit storing up treasures on earth; instead, we share them with needy Christians and trust God to provide for our daily and future needs. It's amazing to see Him provide. In letting go, the paradox is that we take hold of the life that is real life.[95]

Want to join us? To help others to grow in Christian generosity, let it start with you. Martin Luther said: "A man is generous because he trusts God and never doubts that he will always have enough. In contrast, a man is covetous and anxious because he does not trust God. Now faith is the master workman and the motivating force behind the good works of generosity, just as it is in all the other commandments."[96] Are you anxious? Covetous? We were. We still are sometimes. Friends, encouraging Christian generosity is ultimately about growing in faith and humbly pointing others down the same path.

■ 7. STEWARD LEADERS MUST ADMINISTRATE GIFTS HONOR-ABLY BEFORE GOD *AND* MAN. ■

We want to avoid any criticism of the way we administer this liberal gift. For we are taking pains to do what is right, not only in the eyes of the Lord but also in the eyes of man.

—2 Corinthians 8:20–21

---

[95] cf. 1 Timothy 6:17–19.

[96] Martin Luther, *Treatise on Good Works* 3 in *Selected Writings of Martin Luther: 1529–1546,* ed. by Theodore Gerhardt Tappert (Minneapolis: Fortress, 1967), 191.

We return to the topic of gift administration with a fresh twist. In his first letter to the Corinthians, Paul sketched internal processes for taking up the collection. Here Paul appears to share the rationale for such controls: so that the administration of the collection can stand the test of external scrutiny. It must be handled properly before God and man.

In the ancient world, those who handled collections, such as tax collectors and civic leaders, commonly shaved off a portion for themselves. Showing favoritism and taking bribes were also common practices. None of this was to happen with the administration of this collection.

Today, inviting external examination of gift administration and overall financial management takes the form of a financial audit. Most non-profit organizations and churches hire an outside firm to do an audit on an annual basis. If the ministry you serve does not do an annual audit, it should. They should do this not because they do not trust their staff but to build trust with their constituents that their institutional stewardship has integrity.

Additionally, numerous organizations in North America voluntarily welcome the scrutiny of their processes and controls by the Evangelical Council for Financial Accountability. This extra set of eyes helps not only affirm activities are being done in a law-abiding manner before men but also ensures they are God-honoring.

Stewards leaders should discuss this topic with the board to which they report. Statements like the following one from Bob Snyder represent the fruit of such conversations. His board reads a series of eight statements every meeting to reaffirm their commitments, and one relates to stewardship: "We believe those resources God has made available to this ministry should be used in such a way that under the scrutiny of God and others we can be confident that they have been used for the best and highest purposes and projects within the scope of the ministry."[97]

Boards and executives who are steward leaders bless the organizations they serve in following Paul's example and enacting such measures as drafting stewardship statements, submitting to the scrutiny of auditors, and welcoming the oversight of the ECFA. Consequently, they may not

---

[97] Does your organization have a guiding principle on stewardship? This statement is one of the eight *Guiding Principles of International Health Services*. For more information about IHS, visit www.internationalhealthservices.org.

　　　　　　　　　　　　　　　　　　　　　　　　　　BECOMING A STEWARD LEADER

be immune from problems, but they will ensure that gift administration is governed in a manner that is right before God and man.

8. STEWARD LEADERS TEACH THE SPIRITUAL IMPLICATIONS OF EARTHLY GIVING.

> Remember this: Whoever sows sparingly will also reap sparingly, and whoever sows generously will also reap generously.
>
> —2 Corinthians 9:6

The law of the harvest says: what you sow, you reap. Paul adds: "if you sow sparingly, you will reap sparingly." He echoes the thinking of the teacher in Ecclesiastes 11:6, "Sow your seed in the morning, and at evening let your hands not be idle, for you do not know which will succeed, whether this or that, or whether both will do equally well." In using this motif, Paul is not talking about farming; he is teaching the Corinthians that there is a spiritual use for the earthly resources in their possession.

Few modern leaders talk about the spiritual implications for earthly giving better than Randy Alcorn. He sums it up in this way: "Our perspective on and handling of money is a litmus test of our true character. It is an index of our spiritual life. Our stewardship of money tells a deep and consequential story. It forms our biography. In a sense, how we relate to money and possessions is the story of our lives."[98]

What story would your handling of money tell? Would it say you believed life consisted in the abundance of possessions? Would it declare you gave out of a sense of duty or to get something in return? Or would it show you are living this life to prepare for eternity?

For steward leaders, there's a pitfall here. Do not sow truth in hearts because it is a strategy that works to increase giving by a certain percentage annually. One ministry leader I know took this approach. Rather than trying to impart stewardship principles, he decided to just buy copies of Randy Alcorn's book *The Treasure Principle* and give it to his congregation. Did it bear fruit? Sure, because he sowed seed, but much more fruit could have come had he sowed truth into the lives of his people day and night.

---

[98] Randy Alcorn, *Money, Possessions and Eternity* (Wheaton: Tyndale House, 1989), 21–22.

Andy Stanley likewise raises our sights heavenward: "What is given away cannot be taken away. Money invested in God's kingdom is immediately out of reach of the most turbulent of economic conditions. It is the most secure of all investments."[99] Steward Leaders who sow truths like these that teach the spiritual implications of earthly giving help transform the thinking and living of those they serve. You should too, but don't do it because it's a strategy that works. Do it because it positions people to experience the journey of generosity that is both life-changing and eternity-shaping.

■ 9. GOD LOVES CHEERFUL GIVERS WHO REALIZE HE PROVIDES THE RESOURCES FOR GIVING. ■

> Each of you should give what you have decided in your heart to give, not reluctantly or under compulsion, for God loves a cheerful giver. And God is able to bless you abundantly, so that in all things at all times, having all that you need, you will abound in every good work.
> —2 Corinthians 9:7–8

Paul teaches that giving decisions are between you and God, and they are something you must determine in your heart. He also expresses that reluctance should not characterize your giving and compulsion should not influence it. The reason Paul says giving is a spiritual decision between you and God is because God owns everything, He has entrusted stuff to you as a steward, and your orders for its use should come from God alone.

Reluctance and compulsion were realities in the ancient realm of giving. There were responsibilities and expectations tied to being rich. Your duty was to give to the people of your city, and in return, they would provide you with honor and service in reciprocity. Also, if those above you in the hierarchy of authority compelled you to give something, you had to give it, whether you wanted to or not. Understanding this significance before reading this text shows that Paul has again subverted the system. Rather than pulling rank on them and compelling them to give, which they would have done reluctantly, he leaves the giving decision where it belongs—between them and God.

---

[99] Andy Stanley, *Fields of Gold* (Wheaton, IL: Tyndale, 2004), 115.

On this note, I like to remind steward leaders that not only should we *not* care how much a person gives, but also *we cannot care*. If we do, even a little bit, we show that our interactions with people are merely compelling them to our ends. By letting go of the controls, Paul graciously invites the Corinthians *and us* to discover that God is able to provide resources for giving time and time again.

I think we never look more like Christ than when we give from cheerful hearts. Francisco Fernández Carvajal notes, "Our gifts have to spring from a compassionate heart, one that is filled with love for God and other people. Over and above the material value of our gifts we need to keep in mind the importance of our interior disposition. The spirit of true charity is intimately interconnected with a joyful heart."[100]

Are you encouraging people to give from a heart of love, or have you been using coercive tactics to pressure people to give to help you meet your goals? What would an audit of your conversations and your communications reveal?

10. CHRISTIAN GIVING MEETS NEEDS, AND THE EXPRESSIONS OF THANKS BRING GLORY TO GOD.

> Now he who supplies seed to the sower and bread for food will also supply and increase your store of seed and will enlarge the harvest of your righteousness. You will be enriched in every way so that you can be generous on every occasion, and through us your generosity will result in thanksgiving to God. This service that you perform is not only supplying the needs of the Lord's people but is also overflowing in many expressions of thanks to God.
>
> —2 Corinthians 9:10–12

Paul teaches us the two outcomes of Christian giving. Those in need are satisfied, and this service results in expressions of thanks to God.

This entire passage reflects the opposite of what the realm of giving was like in the ancient world *and* what our modern culture pressures us to believe about giving. In Paul's day, the cultural norms dictated that the rich were to do good deeds to those who could give a return, such as service. Resources were deemed as scarce, and the rich were literally

---

[100] Francisco Fernández Carvajal, Volume 5 of *In Conversations with God*, 425.

taught not to give to the destitute because they could not reciprocate. Paul turns these cultural norms upside down, or perhaps, he puts them right side up.

Paul calls the Corinthians to give on every occasion, with an abundance mentality based on the reality that God is the Provider. Paul also does not promise them glory for their giving, as God will be glorified and thanked for their participation. The Corinthians can imitate God's generosity by sharing His resources freely with others. Steward leaders who understand this unleash heaven!

Are your development programs promoting an abundance or scarcity mentality? Are you telling stories of sacrificial giving and sowing truth into the lives of people like Paul did with the Corinthians? Do you need to revisit what you are doing and make some changes? If so, start today.

■ CONCLUSION ■

In this chapter, I tried to explain in twenty minutes what took me twenty years to discern: Just as God's ownership of everything changes how Christians approach giving, understanding that God provides everything changes our role in asking. We do not have to *provide* for the ministries we serve. While trusting God to provide, we get to *proclaim* this profound truth in word and deed—that stewards were made to participate with God in His work with the gifts, goods, and grace they have received from Him.

As Paul mentioned the Macedonians to inspire the Corinthians, I conclude with a story to inspire you. In the 1800s, in Bristol, England, there lived a humble a man named George Mueller, who wanted to care for poor orphans. After studying the Word of God, he chose four rules to guide his steward leadership:[101]

1. He would not receive any fixed salary, both because in the collecting of it there was often much that was at variance with the freewill offering with which God's service is to be maintained and because in the receiving of it there was a danger of placing more dependence on human sources of income than in the living God Himself.

---

[101] Andrew Murray, *George Mueller and the Secret of His Power in Prayer* (Portland: The Prayer Foundation, 2002).

2. He would never ask any human for help, however great the need, but he would make his wants known to the God, who has promised to care for His servants and to hear their prayers.

3. He would take this command (Luke 12:33) literally: "Sell that thou hast and give alms," and never save up money but spend all God entrusted to him on God's poor, on the work of His kingdom.

4. Also, he would take Romans 8:8 literally: "Owe no man anything." He would never buy on credit or be in debt, but he would trust God to provide. While this mode of living was not easy at first, the rewards outweighed the hardships. He testified that it was most blessed in bringing the soul to rest in God and drawing it into closer union with Himself.

Essentially, these rules positioned Mueller to depend on God in good times and bad and to use what he had to attend to God's work, while always sharing any surplus on God's poor. And he avoided debt and trusted God to provide.

Did his ministry flourish? It did in a manner that can only be attributed to the provision of God. Research reveals he received more than $7,200,000 in gifts through prayer, personally cared for more than 10,000 orphans, and rallied hundreds to participate with him in God's work in establishing 117 schools that educated more than 120,000 children in the Christian faith. Like Paul, he taught and modeled what he learned from God's Word: to attend to God's work while trusting God to provide the resources and rallying others to join him.

If your soul is not at rest, might it be because you are trying to *provide* for the ministry you serve? Perhaps God is calling you, like Mueller, to experience "a closer union with Him" by growing in faith to help others grow. That is where this journey has led and continues to lead me.

Gary Hoag

Gary Hoag has been encouraging Christian generosity for more than twenty years, serving in administrative leadership roles at Denver Seminary, Colorado Christian University, and BIOLA University. Today, while working to complete a Ph.D. in New Testament at Trinity College, Bristol, UK, Hoag serves as the Generosity Monk for the Evangelical Free Church of America and the Anglican Mission in America, training pastors and leaders in biblical stewardship and equipping them to model Christian generosity and develop that culture in their local church settings. He also currently provides spiritual and strategic counsel for non-profit organizations such as Prison Fellowship, Providence Network, and International Health Services.

Hoag has authored numerous articles for publications, including *Christianity Today;* co-authored a book entitled *The Sower: Redefining the Ministry of Raising Kingdom Resources;* contributed a chapter to another book, *Revolution in Generosity;* and served as a content reviewer for the NIV *Stewardship Study Bible.* He resides in Colorado with his wife, Jenni, and two teenagers, Sammy and Sophie.

6

THE ESSENCE OF GROWING GIVERS' HEARTS[102]

BY REBEKAH BASINGER

While channel surfing at the end of a long day on the road, I happened upon talk-show host Charlie Rose's interview with Bill and Melinda Gates and Warren Buffet about their Giving Pledge, an initiative aimed at the wealthiest Americans. Despite having achieved professional success beyond their wildest imaginings, the trio's enthusiast comments about giving were proof positive that they've found their greatest significance in giving. Philanthropy has become their vocation, their calling.

Interestingly, what the Gates couple and Mr. Buffet had to say about the place that giving holds in their hearts was remarkably similar to what I hear from the good folks who support the ministry organizations with which I consult. And that makes me happy. I am delighted that joyful generosity is not limited to the super-rich—that it is practiced by givers at every level of the gift pyramid. In fact, individuals of modest or moderate means are the backbone for charitable giving

---

[102] For a more complete exploration of the topic of this chapter, see *Growing Givers' Hearts: Treating Fundraising as Ministry* by Thomas Jeavons and Rebekah Basinger (Jossey-Bass Publishers, 2000). Most of the ideas and some of the content in this chapter originated with that book.

in North America, including for the thousands of organizations that operate under the banner of Jesus Christ.

A gift of just a few dollars can be the entry point to a lifetime of Spirit-inspired generosity. Add passion for a cause to the mix, and it is amazing the extent to which individuals are willing to stretch themselves. Year in and year out, when organizational missions and individuals' interests converge, the miraculous happens.

Unfortunately, in the face of pressing organizational needs and ever-increasing goals, the latest, greatest fundraising techniques trump confidence in God's people to respond to God's call to generosity. Development staff, urged on by impatient boards and frustrated CEOs, race after the next best practice for attracting funds. In the rush to keep up with institutional expectations, donors can be left in the dust or their interests ignored. No one purposefully sets out to hurt the ones who love the organization most or to squelch the God-directed intent of faithful supporters, but it happens.

■ CHARTING A BETTER WAY ■

The good news is that there is a better way. Fundraisers and other organizational leaders can be part of creating relationships through which the act of giving becomes an occasion for faith to grow. An organization's fundraising programs can be structured in the direction of donors' hearts. It is possible to re-vision even a long-standing fundraising effort as ministry. This hopeful message has been the theme of my work over the past twenty years or so and continues to be the driving motivation of my professional life. I am delighted at every opportunity to introduce others to the excitement that comes from helping Christ-followers grow in their understanding of what it means to be rich toward God.

Back in the late 1990s, when I first began talking and writing on this topic, I didn't have many fellow travelers. But what a difference a decade and half has made. Today, there are books, blogs, websites, workshops, degree programs, and entire associations focused on encouraging and equipping fundraisers of faith to think beyond the money. The focus on donors' hearts has even taken hold in some secular circles where researchers and consultants tout the advantages of what is frequently referred to as *mission-centered* fundraising.

For all the talk, however, not much has changed in the way most nonprofit organizations—Christ-centered or otherwise—go about raising funds. Tales of hurts, pressure, and giving fatigue resulting from a relentless barrage of organization-focused appeals are common among ministry donors. Individuals continue to be sought out with the anticipation that they can be persuaded to give to the organization making the contact. Concern for the spiritual development of donors shows up on the priority list as a distant second, if at all.

So I return again in this chapter to a question with which I've been working for more than two decades. What must we do to shape our fundraising efforts in the direction of donors' hearts? My answer is found in attention to three essential confidences.

Growing the heart of the giver comes as we act from and live in confidence in God's abundance, confidence in the generosity of passionate people, and confidence in the call to fundraising as ministry.

■ THREE REASONS WHY GROWING THE HEARTS OF GIVERS MATTERS ■

1. *Seeking to grow generous hearts is good for individuals.* Generosity is a spiritual issue of the heart. A person cannot move toward spiritual maturity until he or she understands that *where your treasure is, there your heart will be also* (See Matthew 6:21).

2. *Seeking to grow generous hearts is good for Christ-centered organizations.* The most vital resource that communities of faith have to do God's work in the world is faithful people. The ministry organization that has re-visioned its development program toward a double bottom line—wherein success is measured in both dollars and heart growth—attracts financial resources, in good economic times and bad.

3. *Seeking to grow generous hearts is good for the wider society.* Faith fuels the American philanthropic engine. According to *Giving USA*, religious households give 87.5 percent of all charitable contributions, averaging over $2,100 in annual contributions to all causes. And being part of a faith community is associated with $1,388 more in an individual's giving per year.

UNPACKING THE THREE ESSENTIALS FOR GROWING THE HEARTS OF GIVERS

▧ CONFIDENCE IN GOD'S ABUNDANCE ▧

Tune in to your favorite news channel, stop by the local coffee shop, or spend an evening with a ministry board of directors. Within minutes, the conversation will likely turn in the direction of the sorry economy and its impact on nations, communities, and organizations. Christ's followers know God has seen worse and that the Lord of the universe is not dismayed by happenings on Planet Earth. But poor-talk has amazing power.

Despite the many promises of God's faithfulness that come to us through Scripture, ministry leaders struggle to remain positive and to maintain their confidence in God's abundance. We say we serve a God who *owns the cattle on a thousand hills.*[103] Our actions, however, convey a very different story to donors, and it is not one of abundance.

It is little wonder when donors become cautious in their giving. They read our letters. They get the message. God is not able, or so the frenzied appeals of cash-strapped ministry organizations suggest. But it doesn't have to be this way.

Christ-centered organizations can be part of putting an end to the destructive attitude of scarcity. When fundraisers present opportunities for donors to respond to God's grace in their lives and to celebrate with the organizations the good work that God will do with gifts provided, there is a chance for hearts to grow bigger. As we walk what we talk about God's abundance, attitudes both within and outside of the organization should begin to change, and exciting heart growth will follow.

Because a wrong understanding of abundance can result in unfortunate actions and attitudes that ultimately reinforce the scarcity mindset, it is important to be clear in our assumptions. God's abundance is not synonymous with getting everything we want, exactly as and when we ask for it. To believe such is a spoiled-child approach to God's abundance. It's akin to treating God like a holy ATM to which Christian's have been given the pin number.

---

[103] Psalm 50:10.

In fact, most of the time God's abundance doesn't come to in the form of money or stuff. Rather, God supplies us with intangible, invaluable gifts such as imagination, patience, an innovative spirit, courage, and wisdom. Living in the confidence of God's abundance means making the most of what we have been given—of learning to appreciate and maximize the worth of what we hold in our hands. This is a lesson that runs across the whole of the Scripture, from God's question to Moses about his staff—"What is that in your hand?"[104]—to Gideon and his ragtag army with their horns and torches[105], to the little boy and his lunch[106], to weary disciples and their fishing nets.[107] The miracle of God's abundance is that the resources we need are already within our grasp.

Unfortunately, as victims of the chronic poor-mouthing that dominates public discourse, we continue to shape our work in the direction of scarcity. Our organizations are caught in a downward spiral of small expectations and even smaller results. The tides of organizational life, the influences of the external culture, and economic pressures are all strong. They can combine and pull even the most determined development team away from the sure ground of confidence in divine sufficiency. We must fight hard against scarcity. Donor-focused development programs must convey a quiet but sure confidence that God is able.

In *Growing Givers' Hearts: Treating Fundraising as Ministry*, Thom Jeavons and I identified three indicators of a fundraising program's movement in a more positive direction. Steward leaders demonstrate their confidence in God's abundance by:

- *Honoring the importance of appropriate goal setting.* I'm not giving away a trade secret by describing the majority of ministry organizations as vision rich and planning poor. Faced with myriad opportunities for doing good, the temptation is strong to overreach in setting fundraising goals. It's up to organizational leaders—beginning with the board—to discern the difference between fundraising targets that challenge supporters to stretch

---

[104] Exodus 4:2.
[105] Judges 7.
[106] John 6:9.
[107] John 21:1–11.

in their giving and goals that are simply beyond the ability of a constituency to achieve.

- *Taking seriously the cumulative negative effect of crisis-centered appeals.* An occasional budget shortfall can be excused, but donors become rightfully frustrated when the ministries they support consistently budget beyond their means. Discouragement grows as year after year, donors hear that once again their giving simply wasn't enough to get the job done—even if that is not what organizational leaders mean to communicate.

- *Maximizing the power of positive thinking and speaking.* Studies show that most people respond most joyfully and generously when there is a ray of light at the end of the organizational tunnel. This doesn't imply spinning our messages or hiding hard truths from constituents. However, in the day-to-day communication with those who care most about our ministries, lifting up the good that's been accomplished with the help of their generous gifts encourages even greater generosity.

▨ SNATCHING ABUNDANCE FROM THE JAWS OF ADVERSITY ▨

I've been impressed by the abundance of good outcomes that can come from rightly dealing with economic difficulties. A financial downturn can be a teachable moment for organizational leaders whose trust is fixed firmly on God's ultimate goodness. Tough times can:

- Open our eyes to the amazing generosity of God's people and help us to be more appreciative of the gifts we receive, regardless of size. When it comes to growing givers' hearts, gratitude is essential.

- Encourage us to work smarter and to maximize every resource available. Donors notice when organizational leaders are wise in stewarding the funds entrusted to them—when gifts are leveraged for even greater kingdom impact.

- Teach us patience and remind us that God's view of time is very different than ours. As we rest in the confidence of God's abundance, we're less inclined to push donors toward hasty decisions that can work against our desire to create faith-encouraging giving experiences.

- Take the focus off of us and our organizations and turn our eyes instead to what God can do through us and our organizations. At the end of the day, abundance comes via the Divine at work in donors' hearts.

Money is important and necessary to mission fulfillment, but to define God's abundance solely in terms of this year's bottom line is to sell short God, the organizations that operate in God's name, and the donors who give as expressions of their faith. The ministry of fund-raising finds life in the realm of God's abundance, where all gifts are overflowing. What a wonderful realization that at the end of the day (or the fiscal year or the campaign), we can step back, take a deep breath, and rest in the confidence that God is able. Donors notice when this happens, and when they do, their hearts grow more confident in God's abundance.

▓ CONFIDENCE IN THE GENEROSITY OF PASSIONATE PEOPLE ▓

Over the past decade or so, philanthropy has become a darling of the popular media. CNN names a hero of the year. The Extreme Home Makeover crew rallies community volunteers to the housing aid of a neighbor in need. Oprah Winfrey has turned acts of charity into a reality show. All the hoop-la suggests that generosity is new to the world. However, as fundraisers know, popular culture is simply catching on to what folks of goodwill have long been doing.

In any community, on any given day, the examples of heart-fueled generosity are too numerous to count. People drop spare change into a jar at the checkout counter to help with the medical expenses of a child with leukemia. Donations of clothes, furnishings, and cash pour in for a family that lost their home in a fire. Volunteers stream into New Orleans; Haiti; Joplin, Missouri; and hundreds of other locales following devastating natural disasters. Strangers stop by K-Mart at Christmas to pay the lay-away bills for needy families. And then there are the mega-donors like the trio with which I began this chapter. Even as the Great Recession drags on, gifts in the amount of the hundreds of millions of dollars continue to be made.

Yet it seems to take more confidence than what many ministry leaders can muster to fall back into the arms of the organization's donors—to believe that if we are faithful in communicating well both before and after the gift, the support base will not let us down. That old Demon Scarcity sneaks up on us, whispering words of fear and cluttering our schedules with activities and techniques for raising funds that get in the way of building relationships with donors. We may not be completely happy with the way things are going. Nor are we seeing the fundraising results we need or desire. But we push on, doing the same things year after year, and then we are surprised when once-loyal donors wander off.

However, confidence in the generosity of passionate people shows itself in the courage to change, to move in new directions. An important first step in growing the hearts of givers is providing opportunities for them to touch and see the work they are supporting—to create a context in which the spark of passion evidenced by a first-time gift or an e-mail inquiry can grow. Ministry organizations with which this happens are intentional about relating to donors and others in ways that allow space and time for God's work in individual hearts. These organizations don't just talk about their work. They give donors a chance to experience it.

This sounds obvious, I know, but I mention it here because too many donors describe themselves as feeling ignored, disrespected, and/ or hungry for follow-up information. Why is this? As I've reflected on this question, I have kept returning to the pressure of organizational goals as the chief culprit. Giving attention to individual donor interests and giving styles is time-consuming, and return on investment by staff isn't immediately obvious. Development offices within small to mid-sized ministries especially struggle to fit donor relations into already over-flowing workloads. However, in today's linked-in world, making time for donors isn't simply optional; it's essential.

When we make time to communicate, with a click of a mouse, would-be givers can research and create their own giving adventures. Connections with causes of the heart are a mere Google search away, eroding the importance of old-time intermediaries. Passionate, generous individuals aren't waiting around for a free spot in a fundraiser's schedule. That's why within organizations that proclaim an interest in growing givers' hearts, staff must be encouraged and rewarded for making room for donors.

Fundraising programs demonstrate confidence in generosity of passionate people by:

- *Trimming the program down to the essentials.* There is no limit of one-more-things that can be done to raise funds for the organizations on whose behalf we serve. If we hope to make room for donors in our schedules and programs, we need to be ruthlessly honest in assessing the return on investment of every activity on our calendars. If we cannot point to how the activity or strategy contributes to growing givers' hearts, we should be open to not including it going forward.
- *Matching fundraising goals to human power available to the organization.* This point is one to which CEOs and boards should give particular attention. There is little to be gained and a lot to be lost by setting goals that require more people-power than the ministry can support. Nothing saps the enthusiasm and passion of a fundraising team more quickly than the struggle of pursuing unrealistic goals year after year. And dispirited development staff are not likely to inspire much joy in donors' hearts.
- *Planning the work and sticking to the plan—but with room to flex in response to donor interests.* Once goals are established, it is up to the development staff to interpret the agreed-upon plans to the right donors, matching organizational priorities and programs with individual passions. Then, as friends of the organization give in support of realizable goals, they share in the satisfaction of ministry achievements—a good feeling that frequently spills over to the benefit of other ministries. A positive experience with one organization almost always builds donor confidence to test the giving waters in another place.

There is tremendous peace in knowing that God is already at work in the hearts of potential donors. The task of the development team and other organizational leaders is to find the intersection between the ministry's mission and the individual's calling. As we rest on the promise of God's abundance and the generosity of God's people, we can press on with confidence and in celebration.

■ A STORY TO ENCOURAGE ■

Here is an example: A fundraising colleague told me about her work with a major donor prospect over a period of more than six months. She had focused the donor in the direction of the project that was at the top of the organization's must-fund list—raising money for AIDS programs in Africa. The fundraiser crafted a beautiful proposal, complete with touching vignettes, photographs, and statistics. But the donor wasn't moved. Instead, the woman wanted to talk about her two grandchildren who had recently been adopted from Bolivia. When she described the joy the little ones had brought to her family, her face simply glowed. Picking up on the woman's passion, the fundraiser said, "Would you be interested in hearing about our work with children in Bolivia?" And so began a wonderful, donor-centered conversation.

Upon returning to her office, the fundraiser prepared a proposal that focused on child health and education programs in Bolivia. It wasn't what she had intended, but it was what the donor had in her heart. The development officer confessed to a twinge of disappointment at the donor's decision. After all, she still had a goal to reach, and she had hoped for a big gift to move her toward it.

Fortunately, the fundraisers understood (and so did her supervisor) that when the focus is on the donor and God's work in his or her heart, there's no such thing as a disappointing ending. Every gift is a cause for celebration, whether or not it matches the agenda of the day. There's always tomorrow and that next visit.

■ CONFIDENCE IN THE CALL TO FUNDRAISING AS MINISTRY ■

Fundraising has only recently earned its stripes as a full-fledged profession, a milestone heralded in the United States by the name change of the National Society of Fundraising Executives to the Association of Fundraising Professionals. Master's level and even a few doctoral programs have sprung up in response to enhanced expectations of development officers. And in many places, the fundraising program has found a place on the CEO's cabinet. So it should not surprise us if development staff, including those working for Christ-centered organizations, are reluctant to think of themselves and their work in anything other than the language of the industry.

However, as has already been stated, fundraising within the community of faith is about more than money or professional standing. To be sure, dollar goals are important and preparation for the job is essential. Resource generation, however, when pursued by people of faith on behalf of organizations that are grounded in faith, is first and foremost about God at work in donor hearts. As such, it is ministry, and those who work as fundraisers in a Christ-centered setting should understand themselves and be understood by others as ministers of God's good news.[108] In other words, fundraising for the Christian development officer is more than a career (a wonderful one, at that). It is a call.[109]

When fundraising is approached as a call, the work flows from a sense of who God is, how God is involved with individuals, and how that involvement shapes attitudes about giving and receiving. Those who make hiring decisions for Christ-centered organizations need to understand that it is impossible for a fundraising program to be shaped as ministry unless the people who are part of the program have been called to the work. And when considering a position on the development team of a ministry organization, it's important that the one seeking the job truly believes that fundraising is more fulfilling to and done better by those who experience themselves as answering a call from God to the ministry of fundraising.

■ AFTER THE CALL ■

That said, a sense of call is merely the beginning. As in any sphere of ministry, there's learning that needs to take place and a lot of hard work ahead. Fundraising as ministry requires both spiritual maturity and professional competence. There's no good in moving forward with one but not the other. The requirements of a first-rate fundraiser in a Christ-centered setting must include all of the skills and professional commitment of any other top-quality development person—and more. When we speak of fundraising as ministry, what we are talking about is new ways—and specifically, theologically sensitive ways—of looking at, assessing, and possibly improving upon the conventional wisdom of the development field. The possibilities presented in the ministry model go well beyond what is hoped for in other fundraising programs.

But how do we maintain confidence in our call, even when others around us don't necessarily think of what we do in that way—or worse, if we are given messages that this is a foolish or wrong-headed way to talk about the work we do? We do so by working in ways that give

---

[108] See Mark L. Vincent's chapter for more on this.
[109] See Gary Hoag's chapter for a deeper discussion of this subject.

testimony to the hope that is within us—the hope that we can raise the funds required and do so in a way that grows givers' hearts.

Fundraisers who are living fully in God's call on their lives and their work:

- *Inspire confidence in others that they are up to the job and that the organization's goals will be met.* They are the ones to whom others look for help in turning good ideas into reality. Even as they seek to master the knowledge and skills necessary for excellence in their professions, they are careful to guard against prideful power games. It takes a servant's heart to grow givers' hearts.

- *Bring out the best in others—be that the CEO, fundraising colleagues, program staff, board members, or donors.* The fundraiser's ministry is one of encouraging, praising, and sometimes prodding (but with a stub-nosed stick) others as they become involved in the development effort. In the short-term, it can be hard to see the return on investment of the effort. Every day, we face the choice of doing (or trying to do) it all ourselves or slowing down long enough to include others in the exciting ministry of fundraising. For those who are confident of their call, the choice is obvious.

- *Are ready and able to fill the gap as stewardship educators.* Researchers report that people of faith are no longer learning about giving in their churches because pastors are reluctant to preach on stewardship topics.[110] By default, the majority of church-goers today are being introduced to the why and how of giving through the ministry of fundraisers representing Christ-centered organizations. The way Christian ministries go about raising money is a powerful form of stewardship education, and fundraisers are stewardship educators, whether the work is thought of as such or not.

Everyone associated with a ministry organization, and most especially those who make decisions about how gift dollars are used, must join in ensuring that the fundraising program is structured in ways that

---

[110] See the chapter from Bishop Leslie and Natalie Francisco for a description of what happens when pastors stop being reluctant.

give attention to heart issues as well as to dollar goals. A right approach to resource generation doesn't just happen. It requires intentionality, organization-wide re-education, and above all, the full commitment of the CEO and the board to re-visioning the fundraising program in the direction of donors' hearts.

▪ CONFRONTING ROADBLOCKS TO FUNDRAISING AS MINISTRY ▪

There is much to be gained from the fundraiser's point of view in approaching our work as a calling. So what's holding us back? As I've talked with people about the challenges of pursuing fundraising as a ministry, the following three roadblocks have shown up in virtually every conversation.

- *The first roadblock is the competence versus commitment myth*—a commonly held bias that professional competency and fervent faith are not compatible. When organizational leaders buy into this myth, they are fearful of straying from the way things have always been done and are suspicious of spiritualizing what they see as secular work. The fundraiser's challenge is to give witness to the fact that when there is a true integration of faith and work, the work is as solid and honorable as the faith. It's not an either/or matter.

- *The second roadblock is the challenge of unreceptive organizational culture* where it's assumed that a ministry-centered approach will limit an organization's ability to reach into new donor markets. Organizational leaders must never underestimate the importance of being true to what the ministry was founded to be. It's the mission and vision of organizations that lead people to work and give on behalf of worthy causes. These are what connect with donors' hearts.

- *The third roadblock is the tyranny of the bottom line.* All too often, fundraisers are handed a goal that has little connection to reality and told to make it happen. The surest way to avoid this trap is good organizational planning. An invitation to be part of "a long obedience in the same direction" (to borrow Frederick Nietzsche's words) is a far more winsome way of describing an organization's priorities than are frenzied pleas for help in *meeting this year's budget.*

The roadblocks are real, but with God's help and the encouragement of colleagues who share our commitment to growing givers' hearts, we can overcome them all. This is the confidence that comes in knowing we are called to the work at hand.

■ CONCLUSIONS ■

"Don't you still believe what you've written about fundraising as ministry?"

The question took me by surprise, coming on the heels of what I thought was a great presentation to a group of CEOs and board members of faith-based nonprofits. Apparently I had not said what this long-time colleague had expected me to say.

I will admit to a bruised ego. Yet my friend's words were what I needed, even if they were not what I expected to hear. Thanks to his prodding, I took time to re-ground myself in the foundational assumptions that undergird my daily work. Now with this chapter, I have the opportunity to invite newcomers and long-time fundraising staff to join me in the exciting ministry of growing the hearts of givers.

A lot has changed over the past couple of decades. However, as a result of returning to the ideas that first fueled my writing those long years ago, I can say with certainty that these things I still believe:

- Any work based on Christian spiritual and moral values and which tries to embody and give witness to them can be a ministry. This includes fundraising.
- Any work or role to which people feel led and in which they feel themselves guided by the Holy Spirit can be a calling or vocation. This includes the role of fundraiser.
- If fundraisers who are themselves people of faith approach donors who are also people of faith in ways that appeal to the best in the donors, touch donors at the level of faith, and reinforce donors' experiences of grace, fundraisers can help donors grow in faith through the act of giving. This is fundraising as ministry.
- If all the people who have a part in raising funds for faith-based organizations (including board members) show as much concern for their donors' spiritual growth as their organizations'

financial needs, they all will help grow donors' hearts. This is the shared reward of fundraising as ministry.

In case you didn't catch my answer to my friend's question, it's a resounding "YES." I am more convinced than ever that approaching fundraising as ministry is the better way—for Christ-centered organizations, for donors, and for development staff. My prayer in writing this chapter is that many other Christian fundraisers will listen for their callings, if they have not already, and consider how they might more fully root themselves in that space of potential blessing where the hearts of the faithful grow more generous toward God and in support of God's purposes on earth.

Rebekah Burch Basinger

R ebekah Burch Basinger is an independent consultant for board development and fundraising, working primarily with theological schools and other faith-based nonprofits. She has served in the administrations of three church-related colleges and also directed a Lilly Endowment-funded project on fundraising effectiveness for the Washington, DC-based Council of Christian Colleges and University. She earned the B.A. degree (1975) in English from Trinity College, Illinois; an M.A. degree (1981) in English from Wichita State University, Kansas; and the Ed.D. degree (1991) in educational leadership and policy studies from Temple University, Philadelphia.

A prolific author, Rebekah has numerous articles on fundraising and board life to her credit and continues to explore these topics through her blog, Generous Matters. She contributed a chapter titled "When Faith and Governance Meet: The Board's Role in Growing Givers' Hearts" to the book, *Revolution in Generosity: Transforming Stewards to be Rich Toward God,* and served as the lead author for "The President's Role in Institutional Advancement" in the Association of Theological School's *Handbook for New Presidents.* She is also the co-author with Thomas Jeavons of *Growing Givers' Hearts: Treating Fundraising as Ministry.*

Rebekah serves on the boards of MOPS International, currently as chair; the Foundation for the Theological College of Zimbabwe; and the Association of Boards in Theological Education. She and her husband, Randall, live in Dillsburg, PA, a short drive from Messiah College, where he is the Provost.

BECOMING A STEWARD LEADER

A (FRUSTRATED BUT HOPEFUL) LAYMAN'S PERSPECTIVE

BY GARY MOORE

I think that what happened in the nineteenth century was that religious leadership in all religions simply abandoned the field of economic morality to the secular world. Religion thus became irrelevant to many people. We helped create a split personality among the business leaders. They could be pious men. They could go to Church or to synagogue or to the mosque, but religion made no demands on them in the marketplace. This separation of personality, I think, is a major tragedy for religion and for the businessman.

—Rabbi Dr. Meir Tamari

Twenty-five years ago, I was a senior vice president of a major Wall Street firm when I hit the wall of Wall Street. I was also the president of my local church and a newer volunteer-planned giving officer for my mainline denomination.

I quickly discovered that my local church and denomination had little interest in planning or giving, if giving is defined as being motivated by the spiritual needs of our members rather than the financial needs of our institutions. I also discovered the church had, and has, virtually no interest in helping more affluent members who might be struggling with the spiritual and ethical dimensions of managing wealth. When speaking for group after group of people like I was, I heard this constant complaint: The church treats us as if we can't get through that old eye of the needle until the annual campaign. Then it treats us as religious royalty.

I can now say with great confidence that the church's split-consciousness is not enriching our religious institutions or our members. True, some churches and ministries occasionally give seminars about managing credit card debt or writing wills. That's good. But one does not have to be a cynical Wall Street veteran to realize such seminars are primarily given to encourage more donations to the church. That is, they are motivated by the same institutional financial self-interest that drives Wall Street and Washington these days. So it struck me and some of my more financially sophisticated friends—the kind who could generously support the church's work as well as the hospitals, colleges, and so on that they now prefer for very major gifts—that even the clergy no longer understand why the Bible says the judgment of a nation begins in the house of the Lord, particularly when it comes to money.

That's why my first counsel the past twenty years to young and seasoned development officers alike was and is this: "Repeat after me, as often as necessary, fundraising is *not* giving, much less stewardship." As another businessman has wisely said, "Philanthropy is about what you do with what you give away; stewardship is what you do with what you keep."

As a result, a friend who is the finance minister of a well-known mega-church tells me I've only had one sermon in the years he's known me. I consider that a compliment. Like Billy Graham, and this is the only way I'm remotely similar to Dr. Graham, I'll develop a new sermon when it seems someone has listened to and applied the old one. The following personal anecdotes, as well as dozens of studies and books I've read during the past twenty years, suggest that this time has not arrived. I pray this does not sound like complaining but like a sincere attempt to help young nonprofit leaders avoid some of the more painful spiritual wounds that I and others have suffered. As the National Conference of Catholic Bishops once confessed in a stewardship pastoral letter, we simply cannot take a reductionist approach to stewardship, as people are growing increasingly sophisticated financially and can sense when we are more interested in their money than their hearts. I have reason to believe we are interested in their money far too often.

BECOMING A STEWARD LEADER

During the nineties, I had the privilege of speaking several times to the old Christian Stewardship Association (CSA), a coalition of a thousand or more evangelical development officers. At one, a well-known leader confided there was nothing about stewardship that he could learn from Roman Catholics. That's precisely why John Stackhouse wrote these words for *Christianity Today*:

> One of the attitudes that is tearing us evangelical Christians apart is the insistence that everyone else better just agree with me when I give my opinion—and if some refuse to do so, then I'll write them off and associate exclusively with those who will. We badly need an attitude of Christian humility that affirms we don't know it all and that we'd like to know more. We badly need an attitude of Christian appreciation, one that recognizes that other people can give us what we do not have ourselves.[111]

That a leader of CSA would be guilty of the closing of the American mind intrigued me. Despite its name, everyone knew CSA talked almost exclusively about fundraising rather than holistic stewardship. In fact, my deal with CSA, as it remains with most of the church, was that I would be a speaker who would *not* talk about fundraising but about all those stewardship concepts beyond it. To be quite honest, I often state I will not talk about fundraising but have affluent friends who still won't come to my talks, as they tell me, "If it's about money and in a church, it's about fundraising." This irony kills fundraising.

In *The Crisis in the Churches: Spiritual Malaise, Fiscal Woe*, Princeton professor Robert Wuthnow wrote: "The steady drop in donations, volunteering, and personal involvement is a direct result of a spiritual crisis—a crisis caused in large part by the clergy's failure to address the vital relationships between faith and money … the solution is not simply to talk more about the financial needs of the Church—30 percent said they would actually give less money if Churches talked more about finances than they do now. The answer is to talk about the broader relationships between faith, work, money, giving, the poor, and economic justice."[112]

---

[111] http://www.christianitytoday.com/ct/1997/october6/7tb035.html. Retrieved 30 December 2011.

[112] *The Crisis in the Churches: Spiritual Malaise, Fiscal Woe* (Oxford University Press, 1997).

As all this was occurring, I was aware that the Interfaith Center for Corporate Responsibility (ICCR), a coalition of three hundred primarily Roman Catholic institutions that steward over one hundred billion dollars, was working on Wall Street to clean up sub-prime mortgage lending. Few evangelicals joined them. I believe a major reason is that *Christianity Today* has said we have such a limited perspective of Christian history that we think of Billy Graham as a church father. That, in turn, causes many of us to put far too much trust in markets and capitalism in general.

Catholics were in business, so to speak, before Adam Smith created modern economics with his book *The Wealth of Nations*. Smith was actually a professor of moral philosophy. Managing the world's wealth was still considered a dimension of theology. So Catholics have the tradition to understand that God has always insisted on favorable lending terms for the needy, rather than charging them even higher interest than the more affluent as capitalism does. Had more evangelicals joined the ICCR in that endeavor, rather than obsess about Y2K, we might have helped to soften the Great Recession. We may have also softened the drop in charitable giving that always occurs during a recession.

I spoke several times at the North American Conference on Christian Philanthropy, a coalition of a thousand mainline stewardship leaders. Despite its name, the stewardship leaders of the mainline churches went beyond philanthropy to at least talk about environmentalism, empowering the poor, socially responsible investing, and so on.

One reason mainline leaders are less effective at fundraising is theological. They simply don't have the urgency to evangelize the world before its imminent end. After he had spent some time in jail actually reading the Bible, Jim Bakker wrote an interesting book about how powerful that concept is in fundraising, despite its being theologically challenged. He added, "I had built my prosperity theology on a few isolated, misinterpreted verses of Scripture ... As I poured over the Word of God, the Holy Spirit used the Scriptures to convince me that I, like so many of my former colleagues, had merely been preaching what I had heard other preachers say. I passed along things I had read in somebody else's books, rather than carefully examining the Scriptures to see what God had to say. I was an unwitting false prophet."[113]

---

[113] *Prosperity and the Coming Apocalypse* (Nashville: Thomas Nelson, 1998).

BECOMING A STEWARD LEADER

Yet my then Episcopal Church was also engaged in *The Decade of Evangelism* during the nineties. When it ended, most Episcopalians didn't know it had occurred. In short, we have so very much to learn from one another, particularly regarding the interplay of morality, economics, and evangelism through the millennia. Sadly, politics often prevent our understanding. They shouldn't.

As explained by Justo Gonzalez in *Faith and Wealth*,[114] a book I'd highly recommend to any person interested in stewardship work, many of the ideas we consider *liberal* derive from ancient Greece, and Plato in particular. As Plato was collectivist in most of his economic thinking, many consider him to be among the world's first communists. He was actually more nuanced. In *The Republic*, he suggested governing elites, who he called "guardians," should not own property, as doing so might conflict with their responsibilities, a sentiment with which Moses rather agreed (Deut. 17:17). Yet Plato also thought it was fine for the common folk to own property. Today, liberals still want the government to provide our health care, retirement incomes, unemployment benefits, and so on.

Many of the ideas we consider *conservative* derive from ancient Rome and philosophers like Cicero. They argued that wealth belongs to private individuals and that we should, therefore, assume responsibility for ourselves. As attested to by the Bible, Romans were not always deeply concerned with their social responsibilities for their neighbors. They were generally skeptical of taxes and thought the only role of government should be to defend the nation's wealth. As the Roman empire expanded, maintaining it became more and more expensive. As also attested to by the Bible, Rome therefore extracted large taxes from conquered nations. But as the legions were spread ever thinner and could despoil no more lands, the legions became a burden on a homeland that demanded security but didn't like taxes to pay for it. You don't have to be an economic historian to see the parallels with today's conservatives.

But there was a third way in those days in Israel. They believed that God, rather than government or individuals, owned all wealth. Perhaps because he knew his people had fallen into slavery in Egypt from Joseph's coziness with Pharaoh,[115] Moses developed an economy

---

[114] Wipf and Stok, 2002.
[115] Genesis 41–47.

where it was the individual's responsibility to care for both his or her self while also caring for his or her neighbors, and particularly for the needy. Due to his experiences in Egypt, Moses commanded his people that "the king is not to have a large number of horses for his army."[116] In that sense, Moses assured Christian faith and practice would always be an equal opportunity offender to the classical ideas of Greece and Rome and to future liberals and conservatives alike.

Perhaps as both Greece and Italy appear bankrupt, which happens when borrowers can no longer pay interest on their accumulated debts, it might be a good time to reflect on our personal *and* social responsibilities, particularly as they relate to interest and other economic matters. Yes, as an investment advisor, I know it's a tough sell just getting people to exercise personal responsibility, much less social responsibility. But there's a reason Churchill said, "Responsibility is the price of greatness." If we want America to be great again, we must practice both. And if we want the church to be great again, it simply must begin by practicing less institutional survival and reassuming the social responsibility of teaching moral economics. Surely we've learned that Washington and Wall Street won't.

We might begin by understanding that America has recently resembled both Greece and Rome. Ever-progressive Washington has assumed more and more responsibilities for us, while ever-conservative Wall Street, both Christian and secular, has resisted assuming any social responsibilities for our affluent nation. Today's libertarians believe America's mixed economy should therefore be replaced by pure capitalism. Some actually believe such capitalism is biblical. They are terribly mistaken. Capitalism may be Christian, but it's hardly biblical. That is, at best, capitalism, as opposed to simple, free markets, and people usually confuse the two, may be the most liberal economic concept in world history, despite our best efforts to baptize it.

In *Mere Christianity*, C.S. Lewis wrote, "There is one bit of advice to us by the ancient heathen Greeks, and by the Jews of the Old Testament and by the great Christian teachers of the Middle Ages, which the modern economic system has completely disobeyed. All these people told us not to lend money at interest; and lending at interest—what we call investment—is the basis of our whole system ... It does not necessarily follow that we are wrong. That is where we need the Christian

---

[116] Deuteronomy 17:15.

economist. But I should not have been honest if I had not told you that three great civilizations had agreed in condemning the very thing on which we have based our whole life."

Perhaps you noticed that Lewis did not say the conservative Romans objected to interest. That may be why, despite all the Bible-based teachings about debt today, I've never heard a conservative financial ministry question the earning of interest. Paying interest, yes; earning it, no. Yet there are still a few Old Order Amish in Pennsylvania who still refuse to earn interest on bank deposits, as do most Muslims. This is how Justo Gonzalez explained the ancient conservative view in *Faith & Wealth*: "All the great writers of Roman antiquity are conservative … Since the earliest of times, the maximum rate had been fixed at 1% simple interest per month, and this was generally the legal limit throughout the history of Roman legislation."

Professor Niall Ferguson confirmed Lewis's perspective of Christian history by writing these words in *The Ascent of Money:* "For Christians, lending money at interest was a sin. Usurers, people who lent money at interest, had been excommunicated by the Third Lateran Council in 1179. Even arguing that usury is not a sin had been condemned as heresy by the Council of Vienna in 1311–12. Christian usurers had to make restitution to the Church before they could be buried on hallowed ground."[117]

It was actually the Protestant Reformers who, correctly in my view, formally legitimated the earning of interest within moral boundaries. As Paul Schervish states in *Wealth and The Will of God:* "Prior to Calvin, the Roman Church and most secular authorities banned usury on two grounds. Philosophically, usury violates Aristotelian precepts, which held that making money on money is a base and unnatural form of profit. Scripturally, many interpreters read Luke 6:35 ('Lend, hoping for nothing again') as outlawing usury … In his own legislation, Calvin outlawed charging interest to the poor; but he allowed interest to be charged in other transactions."[118]

That moral change went a long way in making banking, and therefore modern capitalism, possible. Yet the Reformers always placed moral constraints around such activities. For example, Martin Luther wrote, in his typically blunt manner: "If, after diligent work, his efforts

---

[117] New York: The Penguin Press, 2008.
[118] Bloomington: Indiana University Press, 2010.

fail, he who has borrowed money should and may say to him from whom he has borrowed it: This year I owe you nothing … If you want to have a share in winning, you must also have a share in losing. The money lenders who do not want to put up with these terms are as pious as robbers and murderers."

That moral framework apparently influenced our economic activities until the founding of America.[119] Robert Wuthnow provided this example in *God and Mammon in America*: "In 1639, the elders of the First Church of Boston brought charges against a Puritan merchant named Robert Keayne for dishonoring the name of God. Soon after, he was tried and found guilty by the Commonwealth as well. Writing his memoirs some sixteen years later, he was still stung by the disgrace of the event. His sin was greed. He had sold his wares at a six percent profit, two percent above the maximum allowed."[120]

Only earning six percent would likely get one thrown off a church's endowment board today. That dramatic change over recent decades was explained this way by professor Doug Meeks in *God The Economist*: "The way stewardship is practiced in North America often has little to do with the Bible. It stems primarily from the most influential American theologian, Andrew Carnegie. The Christian religion, Carnegie maintained, becomes pertinent only after production has run its course, money has been made and money has been reinvested. In other words, Carnegie said that Christian faith has to do with charity, and charity does not extend to the questions of economics."[121]

As a result of Carnegie's reducing stewardship to giving, and thereby excluding our faith from our Monday to Saturday economic lives, sociologist George Barna wrote, "Fewer than one out of every ten born again Christians possesses a Biblical worldview that impacts his or her behaviors … The problem with Christianity in America is not the content of the faith, but the failure of its adherents to integrate the principles of the faith into their lifestyles."

In short, while conservative Christians may be politically and socially conservative, we are also quite likely the most liberal Christians in history when it comes to money. We usually understand the liberals have mixed our faith with the political views of atheists like Marx.

---

[119] For more on this, please see Wes Willmer's chapter.

[120] New York: The Free Press, 1994.

[121] Augsburg Fortress: 1989.

But very few realize how much we have been influenced by economic philosophers who have been equally anti-Christian. This is how Greg Forster of the Kern Family Foundation put it in the Summer 2010 edition of the conservative *Claremont Review of Books*:

> Many of the most visible capitalist intellectuals—giants like Milton Freidman, Fredrich Hayek, and Ludwig Von Mises—embraced a new moral case for capitalism that decisively rejected the old one based on the natural and divine significance of the individual. This new moral case was, either explicitly or implicitly, utilitarian and anti-metaphysical.

That materialistic trend has culminated within the church with the development of the prosperity gospel by our newer denominations. Few prosperity ministers seem to have noticed the economic reality described by Jesus when he said our most gracious God "makes it to rain on the just and the unjust."[122] While Jesus said the very purpose of his coming was that we might have life and have it more abundantly[123], he obviously knew that one can be most faithful without growing rich in the material sense. Economic historians say that at the time Jesus spoke of the rich, the average person on earth lived on the equivalent of $500 per year. *The Economist* recently detailed the average person on earth still has a net worth of only $2,200.

I attribute my interest in economic history and reality to grace. In particular, I was blessed with one of those beautiful Southern Baptist mothers who aspired for her son to be the next Billy Graham. I thank God today that she encouraged me as a youth to attend church most faithfully; though, I'd have probably preferred to be playing baseball.

We were lower middle class, but we felt relatively affluent, as it often seemed the testimony of every person who joined our tiny church after being born again resembled a baptized country music song. You can probably hum it: "I lost my job, my wife left me, my dog died, and I drank myself into hell on earth before the Good Lord saved me."

---

[122] Matthew 5:45.
[123] John 10:10.

So you can imagine my surprise when, at age thirty-five and after having achieved the American dream, which included being the president of the Episcopal Church my wife wanted to attend, I hit the wall. The dream was actually a nightmare for my soul. It was the time of Michael Milken's junk bonds and high-paying CDs from savings and loans that hadn't earned a dime in years. After that moral debacle, *The Economist* actually said we should consider the Islamic model, where banking institutions simply pay dividends after profits have been tallied rather than pay interest beforehand. That intrigued me, as I'd never heard the concept in church.

Then the stock market crashed in 1987. I simply did not want to go to work anymore. I was wandering in the desert of despair. But I'd had enough religious training to understand that I no longer knew how to steward: 1) my time from Monday to Saturday; 2) my talent for political science and mathematics and, therefore, the ability to make complex economic matters simpler for people; and 3) the personal treasure I never imagined I would steward one day. So the faith of my youth enabled me to ask the right questions. That is no small thing. It seemed logical that the concept of stewardship should also then help me to find some answers.

I slowly discovered the reductionist ways stewardship is taught in our churches and how they conceal such answers. Those sad ways have since been most ably documented by Laura Nash at Harvard in books such as *Church on Sunday; Work on Monday*.[124] It says: "The Church's often-dismissive response to the layperson's optimistic desire to integrate faith and career cannot be justified. In fact, this attitude may be the largest act of self-marginalization mainstream churches have ever engaged in." In other words, the mainline churches have been committing institutional suicide since they no longer remember stewardship is actually about stewarding the Christian life, meaning 100 percent of our time, talents, and treasures, not just the money we give to church. My experiences affirm Laura's insights.

My Episcopal pastor's idea of stewardship was simply conducting that dreaded once-a-year campaign. We'd pay any outside consultant any amount of money to simply prevent our pastor from talking about money. That's rather ironic if you remember money was a favorite topic of Moses, Jesus, Paul, Calvin, and Wesley. Fully one-third of Luther's

---

[124] Jossey-Bass, 2001.

95 Theses were about the church's abuse of money. But in our church, if people asked to use their time and talents for the Lord, they were invited to lick envelopes in the church office or set up tables in the meeting hall. I might as well have done that for my Rotary Club. I had to anyway, as, unlike my church, it insisted on my attending weekly or attending another club elsewhere. It also insisted on my memorizing The Four Way Test, which is sort of its Golden Rule, and do regular work for the disadvantaged. My pastor rarely suggested anything similar.

Apparently, my pastor was quite typical. After conducting a study of pastors and money for Lilly Endowment, Robert Wuthnow wrote, "When we asked pastors to talk to us about stewardship, we encouraged them to tell us how they understood it in the broadest possible terms. Repeatedly, however, we found the Church was their only frame of reference. They immediately talked about serving the Church, doing Church work, and giving money to the Church."

The fact that our pastors ask way too little of people has been ably discussed by David Murrow in *Why Men Hate Going To Church*. It says, "Many people think the Church asks too much of its members. In reality, it asks too little … Frankly, many Churches have dumbed down Church until it has no meaning at all. We are afraid to ask men for a great commitment, so they think we're after their wallets, not their hearts."[125]

As the president of the church, I was also a confessor figure to the pastor. When telling me he was leaving our little church for a larger one, he was honest enough to confess he needed the larger salary, as that was the base for his retirement pay. I could understand that, as, like most pastors, he was quite underpaid, considering his education, hours worked, and so on. But then he added, "If I don't take care of myself, who will?" I simply remembered he had long assured us that God would. It was then this businessman realized that I too had to prepare budgets just as the church does, but I had enough faith that I did not need to have clients estimate future business with a pledge card.

I have long believed businesses need to operate more faithfully rather than that churches need to operate more businesslike. This could be one area in which we learn from business, however. As my church

---

[125] Nashville: Thomas Nelson, 2011.

still does pledge cards year after year, I know this opinion will particularly irritate many; but I don't believe Americans will ever understand faith should not be confused with church attendance until we get rid of the pledge cards. We might reflect that Mother Teresa once declined a major annual stipend from another organization as she didn't want it interfering with her faith in God to provide. Her ministry never lacked for support.

As a volunteer planned giving officer for my Episcopal diocese, I devoted a Friday afternoon a month to the diocesan stewardship committee. After a year of such meetings, we had decided we would take a "Christ-centered approach to stewardship." That's it! And whatever that was supposed to mean, I quickly discovered few pastors were interested in teaching a literal version of Christ's counsel to sell what we have and give it to the poor, rather than to the church, college, seminary, or evangel. As few pastors have training in true stewardship, most repress that sentiment rather than deal with it in a theologically honest way.

For example, St. Paul wrote that those lay ministers serving churches on the weekend deserve double pay. We also know the workman is worthy of his hire, and early tithes were to be set aside for the needs of the temple priests. But due to the lack of seminary training in stewardship, most pastors are as conflicted over money as my friend the Rev. Dr. Loren Mead. Loren is the seasoned founder of the Alban Institute for Church Growth. But after studying church growth for years, he turned to stewardship education, as he realized all the strategies for church growth in the world won't happen unless Christians are willing to fund them. Sadly, but honestly, Loren has also confessed of what motivated him to make the change:

> Leading the fall stewardship campaign was often uncomfortable for me. I was asking people to pledge to God, but I knew it was coming to me ... Money has more significance in the lives of people than almost anything else. If, indeed, clergy are caught up in debilitating binds over money, they are handicapped in dealing with one of the most significant spiritual problems in their own lives, and they are even more hindered in being of help to those in their congregations who likewise seek to understand what grace and forgiveness have to do with that portion of our lives that we wall off as "money."

I've had other honest pastors tell me they know they begin most stewardship messages with a fib, since we cannot really give anything to God if God truly owns it all. Perhaps we could learn here from financial planners and do away with such emotionalism by suggesting our members rationally allocate God's resources for the various goals we have for ourselves and our world. Considering today's headlines in the financial media, I have to believe they'd understand the importance of funding moral education, assuming we again speak about it.

Other leaders have confessed they can't preach more holistically because they're afraid of offending major supporters of the church or ministry who may be engaged in questionable economic activities. I realized that it should never surprise any of us that Wall Street and Washington subordinate ethics to their pursuit of profit and campaign funds. It might be a good time to remind ourselves that Jesus essentially began the reformation of Judaism by cleansing the temple of the money changers on the very first day of Holy Week. Similarly, Luther was prompted to launch his reformation as he realized the Church had confused fundraising, for St. Peter's basilica no less, with understanding and living the Christian life.

My uneasy feeling only increased when I devoted a cherished weekend a year away from my young son and beautiful wife to attend our national meeting. Year after year, we learned to conduct annual stewardship campaigns, launch the occasional capital campaign for the routine maintenance most organizations do from reserve funds, and discuss the latest techniques for charitable trusts and gift annuities.

One year, I joined the mostly ex-clergy development officers for a beer. If you've heard that anytime you find four Episcopalians you're sure to find a fifth, you can believe it. But that's when you often learn what pastors believe rather than preach. And sure enough, the conversation deepened until they confessed that had old J.P. Morgan not established a generous pension fund for the church, they'd probably have left ministry long ago. Again, not much for us corporate types shackled by golden handcuffs to learn there.

When I returned home and tried to help our churches full of relatively affluent retirees, I discovered most pastors had no interest whatsoever. A couple were honest enough to tell me they didn't want me approaching *their* donors in order to raise money for the diocese, a sentiment with which development officers of colleges, seminaries, and so on are well acquainted. So most of our affluent members set up trusts and such with the help of our local hospitals, colleges, and so on. There was little positive to learn from that approach. When I used charitable instruments on Wall Street to save clients taxes and increase their income, I was considered sophisticated and quite helpful. When I tried to do the same for the church, I was an unwelcome fundraiser.

The national meeting grew so routine that our leader finally asked bored participants what they wanted to discuss. The majority said *socially responsible investing*. That is, even the development officers wanted to discuss more holistic stewardship. Responsible investing was a hot topic in financial circles, and *Christianity Today* had said I wrote the first book on the topic from a biblical perspective. While I won't detail all the passages referring to it, suffice it to say my extended study of the matter indicates there was no asset class of wealth stewarded by the ancients that was not managed with an eye toward the interests of others. In that manner, God rationally assured the massive markets wouldn't create more problems than limited and emotion-based charity could solve. Those passages were summarized by Christ as "love your neighbor as yourself," and he wasn't simply speaking about charity.

Ironically, I wrote the book for the Episcopal Church's stewardship department. When they read the manuscript during the late 1980s, they suggested I have Zondervan publish the book for a wider audience. And it did rather well until evangelicalism grew intrigued with a best seller about an approaching economic earthquake. That other book was the book of the year in conservative Christianity during the time my mentor, Sir John Templeton, who was a Rhodes Scholar in economics and the dean of global investing, was predicting a major bull market due to the collapse of the Berlin Wall and winning of the Cold War, which had been financed with government debt. (To avoid rationalizing more false prophecy, we might remember that by the year 2000, most everyone was projecting our federal debt would be paid off by now.)

The negative economic perspective reduced any interest in socially responsible investing as much as the Independent Sector was saying it was reducing charitable giving. Very simply, fear closes the hand around our money just as surely as greed turns that clinched hand into a fist. That was particularly saddening to me, as the Bible begins by saying that even God had to create wealth before it could be loaned to humanity. If I had the money conservative Christians lost from fear during the early to mid-1990s, and Y2K later on, I could evangelize China.

Furthermore, socially responsible investing has continued to grow into a major counter-trend to an increasingly ethically challenged Wall Street. It might have made our faith more relevant to Americans had the church been seen leading the way in that endeavor. Unfortunately, popular evangelical financial leaders actively resisted the movement, and they still do today. As has been detailed by *Christianity Today,* Ron Blue's investment firm actively resisted responsible investing during the 1990s, and Dave Ramsey's website and investment counselors still discourage it.

That's not to say mainline stewardship leaders have been a help to the responsible investing movement. After hearing his development officers wanted to hear about the more holistic dimensions of Christian stewardship, the head planned giving officer of the Episcopal Church quipped he had to have me speak the next year. But when I went, he talked exclusively about fundraising, capital campaigns, and charitable giving instruments. That was the last year I worked on stewardship with the church, and I then made my agreement to only speak about non-fundraising concepts. After reading of Martin Luther's intense interest in economic morality, I became an Evangelical Lutheran a couple of years later. My experiences since have convinced me that there are many businesspeople like me out there, if some churches, even one church, would simply fill the need.

I had grown to understand that our stewardship department and pastors were actually, if unwittingly, playing a very active role in keeping Christians from understanding the biblical concept. Sure, our pastors generally taught that selfishness was a sure road to death. Yet when talking specifically about money, they seemed exclusively interested in the financial well-being of their institutions and favored projects rather than the financial and spiritual well-being of members and the moral well-being of our markets. While many believe mainline churches are dying due to social liberalism, I'd argue that financial self-centeredness played a major role.

Anyone who studies organizational behavior knows successful organizations usually begin with the vision of an idealistic founder who wants to improve the lives of others. That founder gathers like-minded people who want to do well by doing good. But at some point, most organizations—be they the Episcopal Church, General Motors®, or Lehman Brothers—begin to serve the organization rather than others. They go into decline as those they used to serve lose trust in them and/

or the institutions become irrelevant to the lives of others. The organizations eventually reach a crisis point at which they reform or die.

Notice organizations can survive, even appear to thrive, for quite a while before reality sets in. It's a bit like jumping off a thirty-story building. For twenty-nine stories, it appears there is nothing wrong with your decision. That's simply spending the moral capital and good will built up over previous years and decades, even centuries. It has taken American institutions since the sixties, but I believe many, even capitalism itself, may have fallen to the third or fourth floor today by continuing to pretend stewardship is simply about giving to our churches and ministries.

Unfortunately for church leaders, it is also quite true that it is difficult to remember your objective was to drain the swamp, or teach the holistic stewardship of life, when you are up to your backside in alligators or running a deficit in your organization's budget. So we keep doing the same old things while praying for different results, which Einstein called the definition of insanity.

If you are a volunteer stewardship officer, you should know this will affect your attempts at ministry. The hard reality is that most of today's church leaders are ill-equipped to speak intelligently about money. Seminaries in particular barely touch on the subject. That means two things. First, pastors rarely teach true stewardship. And second, they rarely want anyone else to do so either. While there are certainly exceptions, like the Good $ense ministry of the Willow Creek Association, most prefer for nothing to happen in that critical area of the Christian life rather than taking the chance a lay person might do something wrong. So clericalism is again as large a problem, even in my Evangelical Lutheran Church of all places, as it was when Jesus and Luther launched their reformations.

Our laity make mistakes in music, Sunday school teachings, and so on. Jesus chose laity to be his disciples rather than the credentialed, and Luther taught the priesthood of all believers. So I can only conclude pastors see money as simply too important an area to risk making a mistake. And as any stewardship professional knows, the pastor is the gatekeeper to the congregation. So if you are a lay person, you will usually find the gate solidly locked.

Again, I believe the root of this particular evil bedeviling the church is financial. Jungian psychology may explain it. Jung essentially said we most fear what we have not dealt with in our own souls. That seems particularly true with most professional clergy and money. Many just fear someone other than themselves will make a dollar off the church. The irony is that attitude is killing the funding on which they depend. Apparently, our holistic God, who is quite gracious in the short-term, is also just in the long-term.

As most reading this are likely evangelical financial leaders, I doubt many will miss any mainline denominations that disappear or merge due to financial realities. Still, I've gone into my experiences with the Episcopal Church since the church was once quite influential and very well financed. We might also learn from Robert Schuller's Crystal Cathedral, a now bankrupt television ministry on whose board I served during the years *The Hour of Power* reached multiples of what any other television ministry did. I pray this too does not sound like kiss-and-tell. I continue to respect Bob, imperfect that he is, and I think he respects me, imperfect as I am. Yet, as a former military officer and an investment advisor, I've discovered we humans learn far more from failure than from success.

The first moments I met with Bob before appearing on *The Hour*, he challenged me over an opening statement of my book that said, "As an investment advisor, I can't afford to be an optimist or pessimist. I must be a realist." Bob thought then, as he did the entire time I served on his board, that he needed to be an optimist. The fact that he asked me to run the ministry after it had fallen on difficult times might suggest it is time for all evangelical churches and ministries to be quite realistic. The following lessons I learned while on Bob's board, and the boards of other organizations, might be helpful in that endeavor.

First, like Bob, evangelicalism is heavily dependent on an increasingly expensive and fragmented media. Each media source is growing ever more expensive as it reaches ever fewer people. We may be reaching the point where anyone considering evangelism must seriously wonder if the media is the proper method of doing so, especially if we understand Peter Drucker's teaching that the measure of success in any endeavor is not popularity but changed behavior. We may have to evangelize by living the Christian life.

As on Wall Street, there might be two answers to the question about the media: the short-term answer and the long-term answer. As an investment counselor, I'm often asked if ethics will cost you money or make you money. I simply reply, "Yes". Ethics sometimes cost in the short-term but usually reward in the long-term, but there are no guarantees. Similarly, going electronic might be a short-term stimulus to a stagnant church in need of a mission and a short-term boost to the ego of a pastor suffering burnout, but the long-term consequences need to be evaluated very carefully, particularly from a financial perspective.

Bob may have been the most prolific fundraiser in the history of Christianity. If I've ever met a pastor who had no problem talking about money, it was Bob. He could have easily been the CEO of a major corporation. Bob had actually been quite wise in building a balance sheet that was prudent in its debt-to-equity ratio. But even he referred to the expense of buying air time as *coal money*, meaning our budget of tens of millions each year was quickly burned by buying airtime. What we could hold onto went into buildings. That is, the finances of the Cathedral were quite similar to the finances of most Americans, Washington, and Wall Street firms.

Second, at the very least, we should always, always prudently prepare for economic cycles. We've had fat years and lean years since Joseph's time. Yet it continues to be the fat years that destroy so many organizations, as they assume they will continue forever. When serving as chair of Bob's endowment committee, I was amazed at how little we had for such a large organization. Having legal responsibility for the ministry's properties, I was further concerned that any equity we developed was tied up in highly specialized buildings, the kind that are quite difficult to monetize during periods like the Great Recession. Again, that wasn't the best stewardship model for an affluent-but-spend-thrift America increasingly obsessed with McMansions. Many baby boomer owners are becoming empty nesters, anticipating retirement and in need of less housing.

Third, those choosing to go ahead with media ministries should be particularly sensitive to technological change. Soon after joining the board, I introduced the ministry to a friend who was a global leader in the convergence of broadcast and computer technologies. His counsel was largely ignored until late in the game since the ministry had been successful with television alone.

Fourth, as in the secular world, fads come and go in ministry. Bob's positive thinking was a helpful spiritual antidote to the depressing effects of a secular media operating according to the old newsroom saying, "If it bleeds, it leads. But churches and ministries should always have a laser-like focus on developing the mind of Christ, for as a man thinketh, so is he.[126] And the mind of Christ was realistic if anything. As such, it did not anticipate popularity, fame, or riches for proclaiming the truth about the human condition. The simple reality is that there always has been, and continues to be, a serious tension between popularity and money and true Christianity. That should be of particular concern to those ministries enjoying short-term success by preaching a prosperity gospel.

Fifth, that means we should not rationalize behavior with that of other ministries. God knows you can find a ministry doing most anything today, particularly when it comes to money. As in corporate America, *everyone is doing it* is not a reliable, much less biblical, ethic.

Sixth, and I'm touching the third rail of some ministries here, the boards of major ministries with celebrity leaders simply must deal with who benefits financially when their leader writes books and so forth. The unspoken truth is that many high-profile leaders essentially earn personal gain with what amounts to free advertising paid for by donors. That usually creates considerable unspoken discord within the ministry, particularly when they are heavily staffed with volunteers.

Seventh, never, ever echo the sentiments of politicians that we can separate our personal lives from our professional lives. In my view, Bob made a crucial mistake in accepting the gift of a limousine from a well-intentioned supporter. And I know I was on Bob's board largely due to my friendship with John Templeton, who was a major philanthropist to religious causes. John watched the Hour religiously as he thought it was a spiritual balance to the negativity of the media in general. But being a Calvinist, which means he could make money as long as he didn't enjoy it, John prided himself on driving an old Lincoln. He eventually traded it in, to the relief of many of us, as the driver's door would no longer close. Though he was a billionaire, John bought a Kia® or Hyundai®—I don't remember. And there were times that I'd chat with John about funding a project at the Cathedral that I thought John would be quite interested in, and John would ask if Bob still had his limousine.

Next, and perhaps most importantly, we should be particularly careful of who we grow close to, as in board members. We in business

---

[126] Proverbs 23:7.

realistically know sociopaths often rise to the top of corporations, as their broad smiles mask sharp teeth. Some may therefore bring much-needed financial support at the expense of spiritual loss. Ministers, and particularly those looking for the positive in everything, can be more idealistic about the affluent. It's not been discussed in the media, but I strongly believe Bob's ministry began its descent into bankruptcy the very day he received a significant gift that enabled a major project of questionable value to the ministry. The board had semi-acquiesced to the project by setting a bar for proceeding so high that they thought it would never be reached. But an unknown enabled the project and was immediately put on the board. That board member, whose reputation on Wall Street was for taking over susceptible corporations, almost immediately launched a hostile take-over of the ministry.

I, therefore, believe board members absolutely, positively must look gift horses in the mouth. At best, board development commit-tees should always understand those affluent who are often sought for boards are not always religious royalty but in greater need of spiritual guidance than others might be. The more they are able to give, the more they may need spiritual guidance. For example, Ken Lay of Enron served on Bob's board as I was joining it. I never met him, but my fellow board members thought highly of Ken. He gave generously, as he did to his local church and other organizations. But only the most conflicted among us will remember Ken as a great Christian steward. While you'll rarely hear this from a ministry, even B.C. Forbes, the founder of the magazine that celebrates wealth, once wrote:

> Too few millionaires who aspire to win fame as philanthropists begin at home, among their own workers. To grind employees and then donate a million dollars to perpetuate his name is not a particularly laudable record for any moan to live or to leave behind him. Of course, it is more spectacular, it makes more of a splash to do the grandiose act in sight of all men, where it will be read of and talked of. But it is rather a pitiable form of philanthropy.

Ninth, when we are fortunate enough to establish and nurture a relationship with a major donor who has both the financial and spiri-tual ability to take our ministry to its next level and the willingness to do so, we do not want to waste it. Late in my board service to the Cathedral and *Hour*, we needed to make a change in a mission-critical board position. Bob approached an old friend who had been relatively generous with money and expertise. Due to various reasons, the friend couldn't accept the position. But he wrote a million-dollar check to the ministry.

Bob reported the gentleman couldn't accept the position offered and quipped anytime we didn't want to assume a major responsibility, a million-dollar check would excuse us. He may have been joking. I wasn't sure. But I remember thinking about how the gentleman was investing hundreds of millions of dollars into ventures close to his heart. And he had a heart for moral economics at a time our corporations and Wall Street desperately needed his perspective. In short, I thought Bob settled for far too little. That was exactly what David Murrow said in his book about men hating church, as it usually asks too little of them.

Finally, be sensitive to the ethics of managing *all* of the ministry's assets, including endowment and retirement funds. Jesus said our hearts will always be where our treasures are.[127] Most ministers mistakenly interpret that as where our tithes and gifts are. But Jesus knew better. Give money to a ministry to fight casino gambling but invest your IRA in casino stocks and see if you're not happy when casinos are more profitable in the future. The fact that most of us invest in what we used to preach against just might be the greatest cause of cultural Christianity today. As Billy Graham has said, if we get our money right, everything else just falls in line. I was strongly rebuffed at both Bob's and a college board I once served on when I tried to get the endowment committee to get the seemingly small, but actually huge, thing about the ethics of our endowment funds correct. So it was easier for both to be less than faithful with larger things.

By this point, you should be wondering why I am more hopeful for the future than I've been during the thirty years I've been doing stewardship work in the church. Very simply, I believe the Bible and my experiences on Wall Street affirm the old saying that it's always darkest just before the dawn. And there is considerable evidence, from quite disinterested parties at that, that America might soon remember why our money contains the phrase "In God We Trust."

---

[127] Matthew 6:21.

Consider for example that *The Wall Street Journal* recently said: "The Benefits of the Bust: The financial crisis is leading to a new model of capitalism ... The propensity of modern economic theory for unjustified and over-simplified assumptions allowed politicians, regulators and bankers to create for themselves the imaginary world of market fundamentalist ideology, if government will only step aside. Although the academic recommendations from the Left and Right differed in almost every particular, including on stimulus spending, they had one striking feature in common—a detachment from reality that made them completely useless for all practical purposes."

Professor Robert Fogel, a Nobel laureate in economics and a religious skeptic, recently wrote a book entitled *The Fourth Great Awakening*.[128] It predicts that due to the failures of both left and right, we are at the dawn of yet another awakening that will not only be spiritual, as many in the church even seem to believe, but traditionally religious. He adds: "One cannot understand current political or ethical trends, or properly forecast future economic developments, without understanding the cycles in religious feelings in American history." So it could be good news for both the church and the economy that the two senior editors of *The Economist* magazine, only one of which is a believer, recently co-authored a book entitled *God Is Back*.[129]

Professor James Buchanan, another Nobel laureate in economics, echoed the need to look up rather than left and right when he told *The Wall Street Journal*: "The loss of faith in politics has not been accompanied by any demonstrable faith in markets. We are left, therefore, with what is essentially an attitude of nihilism toward economic organization. There seems to be no widely shared organizing principle upon which persons can begin to think about the operations of a political economy."

Peter Drucker, being ever prophetic, anticipated Buchanan's frustration during the mid-1990s and wrote *Post-Capitalist Society*.[130] Peter, as he liked to be called, wrote, "Every few hundred years in Western history there occurs a sharp transformation. We are currently living through just such a transformation ... Political and social theory,

---

[128] University of Chicago Press, 2000.
[129] New York: Penguin Press, 2009.
[130] HarperBusiness, 1993.

since Plato and Aristotle, has focused on power. But responsibility must be the principle which informs and organizes the post-capitalist society. The society of organizations, the knowledge society, demands a responsibility-based organization."

Perhaps you've noticed that Budweiser® is now using the slogan, "Drink responsibly" and Liberty Mutual Insurance Company is using the slogan, "Responsibility is our policy." The leaders of Citicorp® have spoken of *responsible banking.*

As economically encouraging as that might be, we in ministry should remember that not only was Peter Drucker a prophetic management guru, but also he once taught theology. So his statement was likely far more religious than most of us might assume. Peter likely knew that Richard Niebuhr once wrote a book entitled *The Responsible Self*[131] that said, "There are doubtless as many ways of associating Jesus Christ with the responsible life as there have been ways of associating him with the ideal life or the obedient or dutiful one ... The Christian ethos so uniquely exemplified in Christ himself is an ethics of universal responsibility."

Very simply, we believe Christ never created a single problem on earth, or committed a sin, yet he accepted responsibility for all the world's sins on the cross. Due to humanistic philosophies, that is exactly the opposite of what we have gotten from Wall Street and Washington recently. I have yet to hear anyone accept any responsibility for our economy nearly imploding during the Great Recession.

That is the easy confession, however, as it is about taking the specks from the eyes of others. The much more difficult confession involves taking the logs from our own eyes. I have also never heard a major Christian leader accept responsibility for any of our economic problems, but we surely have many sins of omission, and even commission, to confess. We can help America to look up rather than right and left only by re-assuming our God-given responsibilities for creating the more abundant life, which is both spiritual and material.

After all, that's why Jesus himself said he came to earth. Luther knew that. We could do worse than imitate both.

---

[131] Harper and Row, 1963.

Gary Moore

Gary Moore is the founder of The Financial Seminary. He has a degree in political science, was a senior vice president with Paine Webber, and has written five books on morality and political economy, the last being *Faithful Finances 101* from the John Templeton Foundation Press. His next book, expected early 2012, is *Look Up, America!* His website is www.financialseminary.org.

AFTERWORD: STEWARDS FOR GOOD— ON BECOMING A MORE CONFIDENT STEWARDSHIP LEADER

BY DAVID J. LOSE

This book was intended to change your life, both your life as a Christian steward and your life as a leader of other Christian stewards. If it hasn't, you may want to ask for your money back. Before you write that e-mail, however, I want you to ask yourself whether or not you have truly opened yourself to being changed. Some changes in life—the loss of a job, the death of a loved one—we have no control over. Many others, however—starting a healthy diet, exercising, cutting back on television, or spending more time with family—are entirely within our control. Being a more intentional steward and leading others in more faithful stewardship is decidedly part of the latter category. This is a change we may contemplate but do not have to make. And year after year, many of us simply don't.

Why not? Why don't we grab the bull by the horns and put our people on notice that as Christian leaders one of our primary responsibilities is to invite them to examine how they use the resources with which God has entrusted them in light of the gospel of Jesus Christ? From my experience as a Christian leader who once dreaded talking about the life of the steward, I can appreciate several reasons why many of us may find it difficult to talk about money. I also can share what changed in my life and ministry to make me look forward to those conversations.[132]

■ SOURCES OF OUR STEWARDSHIP ANXIETIES ■

First, it may be that deep down we are not confident that other people's stewardship is really our business. Oh, we know we're supposed to encourage them to be cheerful givers, but we hesitate to say that stewardship—and, yes, that includes the way they spend their money—is ultimately a matter of Christian identity and obedience. After all, we've been coached by the culture—both inside and outside the church—to believe that certain things are private and therefore not open to public discussion. Given that the top three subjects in this category are most likely religion, money, and sex, it is little wonder we hesitate to talk about stewardship, as in one fell swoop we tackle two of the three unmentionable topics!

Further, we may be nervous about exposing our own giving to public scrutiny. Depending on where we are in our careers (paying off student debt, putting our kids through college, preparing for retirement), our situations may leave us struggling to make significant gifts. Even if we are devoting a healthy portion of our income to giving, we may feel insecure about whether or not the amount is sufficient to qualify us as models of Christian stewardship.

Finally, we may worry that our efforts will appear to be motivated by self-interest, as many of us draw salaries from organizations that count on the gifts of those we are charged with motivating to give. I have heard numerous pastors and organizational leaders say that the tension they feel around asking people for money is among the most disagreeable aspects of ministry.

These are understandable causes of trepidation over discussing the life of the steward, but I learned they are not reasons to relegate it to other staff, to employ secular fundraising methods that have little or no connection to Christian faith, or to avoid linking the life of the steward to our identity as followers of Jesus Christ. What changed my attitude—thanks in large measure to the candor of many faithful

---

[132] I realize that stewardship is much larger than "money," but for a variety of reasons, most of us are much more comfortable talking about stewarding our "time" and "talents" than we are our "treasure," and so I will focus my comments on our stewardship of our monetary wealth.

parishioners—were three important discoveries that underscore key ideas found in this book.

◼ STEWARDSHIP DISCOVERIES ◼

1) Stewardship isn't really about money but instead is about identity and values.

We have two kinds of values. Our stated, conscious values stem directly from our identity and are those we name out loud when we talk about things that are really important to us. In addition to these stated, identity-driven values, however, we have operative values, the ones that guide our behavior on a day-to-day basis. While we may not always be aware of them, they have a powerful impact on our actions in the world.

I can almost hear you protest, "shouldn't these be the same?" Ideally, yes; but often they are not. The slight lurch of your stomach each time you charge a purchase that exceeds what you promised yourself you would spend tells you so. You know that feeling, and so do I. It indicates something got in the way of our stated values and led us to act in ways not true to ourselves. It may be that we were caught up in the cultural penchant to equate possessions with status or, more perniciously, with happiness. It may be that we spent money to make ourselves feel better when we felt stressed or down. It may be that that buying something felt like an accomplishment.

Whatever the reason, our actual behavior does not always reflect our stated values. This dissonance troubles many of us, as we sense our Christian identity slowly eroding away. Recall, for a moment, the parable of the rich fool.[133] What is interesting about this parable is that it makes little sense at first glance. This man is not a cheat. He is not a thief. He is not even particularly greedy. He worked hard and made a lot of money, just as most of us dream of doing. So what was his mistake? Ultimately, it was about his identity. He went astray by believing his wealth secured his future and made him independent—not only from personal need but also from others and from God, both of whom he never mentions. His identity stems not from his relationships with God and neighbors but from his wealth and the illusion of security and independence that wealth creates.

---

[133] Luke 12:13–21.

I regularly catch myself doing something quite similar, dreaming that, *If I just had a little more in the bank, or if the mortgage were paid off, or if the cash for the kids' college education was already saved, or [and here, fill in the blank] ... everything will be okay.* The allure of money is that it creates the illusion of independence. It promises us that we and the organizations we serve can transcend the everyday vulnerabilities and needs that remind us that we are mortal, created beings who are ultimately and always dependent on the provision of God. Conversation about the life of the steward is essential because it reminds us that money, while a convenient medium of exchange and powerful economic tool, makes a poor idol. We must take care lest money becomes a false god.[134]

2) People are more eager to talk about stewardship than we often imagine.

This was the perhaps the biggest shock of my early ministry, as I assumed most people did not like stewardship conversations. I was wrong, in part. Yes, we live in a culture that frowns upon discussions of money, and our congregations and other Christian institutions are rarely an exception. As Robert Wuthnow writes, sharing the results of a three-year study of Christian attitudes about money, "In the survey 89 percent said they never or hardly ever discussed their family budget with people outside their immediate family. The proportion who seldom discussed personal finances with fellow Church people was even higher—97 percent."[135]

Part of this reflects a culture in which money and faith have been remarkably compartmentalized.[136] And part of it reflects skepticism directed at the motives held by Christian leaders when preaching and teaching about stewardship.[137] At the same time, however, most

---

[134] See Mark L. Vincent's discussion on the god-like power of money in his chapter.

[135] Robert Wuthnow, "Pious Materialism: How Americans View Faith and Money," *The Christian Century*, March 3, 1993, pp. 239–242. (This article can be found online at: http://www.religion-online.org/showarticle.asp?title=238.)

[136] Wuthow, again: "Money is allegedly value-free. It is simply a convenient mechanism of social exchange. Indeed, 68 percent in the survey agreed that 'money is one thing, morals and values are completely separate.'" (*Ibid.*)

[137] "Many people believe that Churches should be devoted entirely to the spiritual life, rather than having to pay any attention to material needs. In the survey 43 percent agreed that 'Churches are too eager to get your time and money.' On another question, 36 percent said 'it annoys me when Churches are too eager to get your time and money." (*Ibid.*)

Christians harbor deep concerns about money and materialism. As Wuthnow writes, "In the survey, 89 percent agreed that 'our society is much too materialistic'; 74 percent said materialism is a serious social problem; and 71 percent said society would be better off if less emphasis were placed on money." As I found through numerous conversations with parishioners over the years, similarly large percentages report worrying about how their children will handle money and how financial concerns strain their relationships. These subjects are willingly discussed.[138]

In discussing these subjects, we make the link between money and values, and particularly the dissonance between our stated and operative values. It is critical and helpful for us to do so. Numerous studies have shown that when people leave congregations, it is usually not to attend some other church but rather because they believe the faith has little to offer them as they seek to navigate the challenges of day-to-day life.[139, 140]

So perhaps I should not have been as surprised as I was when parishioners thanked me for bringing up something that is a huge part of their lives. Open, honest conversation about our role as God's stewards, about the challenges of viewing and using money in a healthy and faithful way, and about our responsibility to use money and all of our gifts in a way that honors God and respects our neighbors, provides people with a biblical and theological framework to help them make sense of an important and pervasive aspect of their lives. It provides them one more way of connecting their faith lives on Sunday morning with the rest of their lives and work in the world Monday through Saturday.

Further, we need to recognize that there are many, many voices seeking to influence the spending habits and views about money of the adults and children in our congregations, and they seldom have the best interests of our people at heart. Articulating a vibrant theology of stewardship provides an important alternative to the cultural voices

---

[138] The chapters written by Gary Hoag and Rebekah Basinger push out the importance of focusing on the giver's heart.

[139] See, for instance, Wade Clark Roof, *Community and Commitment* (New York: Elsevier North-Holland, Inc., 1978), 33–34; Mark Chaves, *Congregations in America* (Cambridge: Harvard University Press, 2004), 34; and Ward Clark Roof and William McKinney, *American Mainline Religion: Its Changing Shape and Future* (New Brunswick, NJ: Rutgers University Press, 1987), 236–243.

[140] The chapters written by Wes Willmer and Leslie and Natalie Francisco push out the importance of the local church as a center for these conversations.

about money. And keep in mind that the opposite is true as well: to *not* talk about the relationship between faith and money sends the signal that faith doesn't apply to our economic lives, leaves the cultural voices unchallenged, and ends up accentuating the gap many already feel between church and the "real" world.

3) Stewardship conversations often lead to deeper confidence in the gospel.

There is little question that one of the most dominant misperceptions stewardship leaders must overcome is that stewardship is about fundraising. Or, to put it more crassly, that whenever Christian leaders talk about stewardship what they are really after is your money. One way to do that is, as we discussed above, to shift stewardship conversations from asking for money to helping people think about their financial resources and decisions in light of their faith. Another is to invite people to recognize that, because of the importance of wealth in our culture, developing a healthy attitude about money is often the key to a deeper and richer life.

At first, this may sound foreign to a culture that accepts the premise that more money equates more personal happiness and organizational success. Over time, however, through study and application of Scripture in daily life, even the most intractable views can be transformed.[141] Consider, for example, the economic implications of the first line of Psalm 23, arguably the best known verse in the Psalms and perhaps the whole of the Old Testament: "The Lord in my shepherd and I shall not want." As a backdrop to this Psalm, consider how powerful *wanting* is in our culture. Consumer spending now accounts for nearly 70 percent of our gross domestic product (GDP), which is significantly higher than most other industrialized nations (European countries average closer to 50 percent, and during our parents' era, it was closer to 60 percent). That's right: more than ever before, our economy is powered by our collective nights out to dinner, trips to the grocery store, and occasional shopping sprees. And to make that all work we are encouraged at every turn to *want*: to want *more* stuff, to want *nicer* stuff, to want *lots* of stuff.

We live with an imagination dominated by a pervasive sense of scarcity, far more aware of what we do not have personally and organizationally—and therefore should go out and buy—than what we do have. We are consumed by what we lack instead of grateful for our

---

[141] For more on this, see Scott Rodin's chapter.

abundance. We are driven to get more instead of content to celebrate enough. And we measure ourselves against deficits instead of glorying in our gifts and blessings—our assets.

This is where careful study of Psalm 23 comes in. As Old Testament scholar Clinton J. McCann points out, at every turn, Psalm 23 promises us God's providence and provision of everything we need in this life.[142] Yet, as the statistics Wuthnow shares about our economic concerns demonstrate, somehow we forget this. Part of the issue is the consumer-oriented culture in which we live. Bombarded by 24/7 advertising that seeks always to make us aware of what we don't have, it is easy to be seduced into thinking that happiness comes from getting everything you want instead of recognizing and wanting all that you already have.

I suspect Christian leaders must shoulder some of the blame. When stewardship conversations are dominated by requests for money, we feed the popular assumption that if we or our organizations had more, then we could be satisfied. Yet Psalm 23 invites an alternative mindset with its simple, singular, and salutary affirmation: "The Lord is my shepherd, I shall not want." That is, *the Lord is my shepherd and provides all I need.* Period. Interpreted this way, Psalm 23 simultaneously challenges the cultural assumption that the path to happiness is paved with gift cards, while inviting a trust in God's providence that creates confidence and contentment that is as precious as it is rare. Most of our people, I discovered, are eager, even hungry, for such Bible study and conversation. It liberates them from dominating and destroying attitudes about money, sufficiency, and self-worth.

■ CONCRETE SUGGESTIONS ■

Armed with these discoveries, I ventured forth into more intentional stewardship teaching and preaching. Before long, I began to enjoy it. Here are a few of the most important lessons I learned along the way.

1) *Make the life of the steward a consistent part of the message.* The only way to help all of us realize that stewardship is not fundraising but rather is part and parcel of our Christian identity is to make it a part of our regular planning, preaching, teaching, and

---

[142] Commentary on Psalm 23, from WorkingPreacher.org: http://www.workingpreacher.org/preaching_print.aspx?commentary_id=578t.

conversation. If the only stewardship conversation is in relationship to the annual budget, it feeds popular misconceptions and misses the opportunity to help people recognize the important connection between their spiritual and economic lives.

2) *Tell people about the difference their stewardship is making.* Talking about stewardship is not just asking people to give. It is also about showing people what is being accomplished through their stewardship, both inside and outside of the organization. By affirming what their lives as stewards accomplish, you actually affirm and confirm people in their identity as Christian stewards.

3) *Disconnect stewardship conversations from requests for financial support.* Of course, there is a time and place to ask people to give money. I find, however, that as people discover the ways their faith helps them navigate our materialistic culture with greater confidence and fidelity, their generosity soars. Helping them recognize that their congregation and other Christian organizations are resources for them to make sense of their economic lives in light of their faith may be the most under-utilized and important aspect of service rendered by steward leaders.

4) *You do not have to do this all alone.* You and the organization you serve will be much better off if you stop trying to do it alone. I will never forget the year the chair of our stewardship committee ended her role. She had planned to resign her position because she felt like a hypocrite asking others to give when she knew she would have to reduce her pledge significantly. But when she explained to the church council why she was resigning, another member said, "That's okay. We know you can't give as much this year, so we're giving more. That's what families do." Trust me, when she shared this story with the congregation, her words were far more powerful than any of the sermons I preached that year.

5) *Be honest about your concerns and struggles.* Candor speaks powerfully. If you are worried that by talking about opportunities to give you will appear self-serving, say it. If you struggle with decisions about how much to give, admit it. If you wonder

about how your spending reflects your Christian identity and values, talk about it. Your open naming of these issues not only makes you a more sincere, and therefore more trustworthy, steward leader, it also models for others the challenging and rewarding work of connecting faith and money.

As I said at the outset of this piece, the essays in this collection were written to help you transform your life as steward and leader. I hope they have done so. In order for that transformation to happen, you need an open heart. You also need, however, a willingness to have your view of these matters transformed and a willingness to try new strategies, to embrace new practices, to experiment with new approaches. That can be both an exciting and daunting venture. As you enter into it, know how appreciative we are for your faithful struggle to be the kind of steward leader that the church of Jesus Christ needs. Thank you. Even more, thank God for you.

David J. Lose

David J. Lose holds the Marbury Anderson Chair in Biblical Preacher at Luther Seminary, St. Paul, MN, where he has previously served as Academic Dean and now directs the Center for Biblical Preaching. Lose is the author of *Making Sense of Scripture* (Augsburg, 2009), *Making Sense of the Christian Faith* (2010), and *Making Sense of the Cross* (2011). He speaks nationally and internationally on matters of preaching, biblical interpretation, stewardship, and the relevance of the Christian faith in a postmodern world.

CHRISTIAN LEADERSHIP
ALLIANCE

To order additional copies of this book, call:
(949) 487-0900
or please visit our online bookstore at
www.christianleadershipalliance.org